Hippie War

Battle for the
Harrisonville Square

Hippie War
Battle for the Harrisonville Square

Jonathan A Jones

This book is dedicated to
Frankie Wirt, Donald Marler
and Orville Allen, who died on
that fateful day in 1972.

Hippie War: Battle for the Harrisonville Square
2023 Edition
©2023 Jonathan Jones, All Rights Reserved
Printed and bound in the United States of American

For information contact Floating Spark Publishing
1660 N Hunter Dr
Olathe, KS 66061
www.JonathanJonesAuthor.com

admin@JonathanJonesAuthor.com

Available in these formats:
ISBN: 979-8-9874297-0-9 (Paperback)
ISBN: 979-8-9874297-1-6 (Kindle)
ISBN: 979-8-9874297-2-3 (E-Book)

Library of Congress Control Number: 2023902998

Although the author and publisher have made every effort to ensure the accuracy and completeness of the information contained in this book, we assume no responsibility for errors, inaccuracies, and omissions, or any inconsistency herein. Any slights of people, places, or organizations are unintentional.

Acknowledgements

Jill Jones
Jennifer Healy, Editor
Polly Blair, Editor
Cass County Historical Society
Cass County Library
Allen Family
Marler Family
Wirtz Family

Special Thanks

There are too many people that I interviewed to thank them here. Their names, if they wanted them to appear, can be found in the references section at the back of the book. I would like to offer a special thanks to a few people who went above and beyond to help me gather information.

David Atkinson
Kathryn Hackett
John Hofer
Rita Simpson-Inman
Sharon Smith
Janice Street

Advanced Readers
Matt Brown
Janice Street

Contents

Preface

It would be dishonest of me to say that I remember the events that took place on that April day in 1972. I was six years old and lived in a peaceful neighborhood on a peaceful Harrisonville street three miles away from the city square where the action in this story occurred. Growing up in Harrisonville, I have always found this story fascinating in the way that a young man finds bloody local history fascinating, particularly when it happens in his hometown.

I read the book, ***Charlie Simpson's Apocalypse***, in my late teens but many years passed before I thought of it again. In 2021 I had written a couple of books about local civil war history and was also publishing a local history blog on my website, www.JonathanJonesAuthor.com. While searching for a new topic for my next blog post, my wife suggested writing about the shootings on the Harrisonville Square. I immediately set about reacquainting myself with the story. A plan for one 500-word blog post turned into four installments of about 1,000 words each. The tremendous interest that these posts generated made me think that it might be worth considering a book project centering around the event.

I was still on the fence about pursuing this as a project when on Saturday, April 16th, 2022, my wife, Jill, and I were in Harrisonville where I was presenting a program on one of my previous books to a group at the local library. I had mentioned to Jill that after the meeting I wanted to go east to the Chilhowie area to try and find Charlie Simpson's grave so I could take a picture to include in my blog series. I had found the location of his grave online and felt sure that I could find it if we went out and looked. The actual cemetery is in the middle of nowhere, several miles down multiple gravel roads, the kind of place where the only way you end up there is if you wanted to end up there.

After initially going to the wrong cemetery, we figured out our error and eventually arrived at the correct cemetery. The cemetery is small, maybe one hundred graves or so, and located in between several farms on a long stretch of gravel road. Walking into the cemetery, I noticed a solitary woman sitting in front of a grave. She turned and looked at us, probably wondering what anyone else was doing in this lonely spot and asked if she could help us find a grave. I responded that I was looking for the grave of Charles R. Simpson. She immediately pointed to the grave at which she had been sitting. After a little more discussion, we discovered that she was the publicly unknown daughter of Charles R. Simpson.

What!

There is no mention in any existing documentation that Charlie Simpson had a daughter. After speaking with her for quite a while, we found out that she was adopted at birth in 1970 and only recently had been able to piece together the identity of her mother after her adoption records were unsealed. Her biological father was not listed on the original birth certificate. She was able to figure out his identity with the assistance of a newfound relationship with her biological mother and DNA results. Charlie Simpson's daughter informed us that this was the first time that she had visited the cemetery after learning of the identity of her biological father.

The chances of us meeting this person, with this background, in this place, at this time, have to be a million to one. Through Charlie's daughter, I was able to reach out to her mother during the research for the book and some of the information from that discussion is included in the story I am about to tell. That coincidence was the clincher. I knew at that point that I had to tell the story.

The shooting on the Harrisonville Square happened fifty years ago. I have done my best to pull together all newspaper accounts, as well as the Rolling Stone article and the subsequent book, ***Charlie Simpson's Apocalypse***, both written by reporter and writer, Joe Eszterhas. I have also interviewed many residents, former residents, family members, former police officers, and others who were either directly involved or had some relationship with someone who was directly involved. Several of the people that I spoke with did not want their names included in this book. I have respected their wishes and they are listed as anonymous sources in the reference section at the back of this book. It should be noted that many of the people I reached out to wanted nothing to do with me or this project.

Much of what is in the sources authored by Joe Eszterhas is secondhand information. In his writing he related incidents told to him by some of the hippies with no way to verify the accuracy of the information. In his defense, some of the stories would have been difficult to verify, even though he was in town shortly after the shootings. The adversarial nature of the situation in Harrisonville at the time, meant that once you were labeled as being on one side or the other, you would not get the time of day from the opposite side. Also, be aware that some of the quotes from the article and book are very likely the ramblings of the hippies as they sat with Eszterhas drinking alcohol and smoking weed. That does not mean that everything from Eszterhas is not true, it just means that some of it should be taken with a grain of salt. Readers should understand that the truth from that source may have been stretched a bit while getting high around a bonfire in a field outside of town.

Through my research into the story, I have learned some things that I think were largely unknown before this book. I have also learned that some of the common facts of the situation were incorrectly reported by many media outlets. This is a story with two distinct versions: the hippie version and the local authority's view. Fifty years later, the best we can do is to try and piece the truth together based on the stories that come from the participants on both sides. Add to that the stories told by those who were not directly involved but were sitting on the sidelines watching the events unfold. My goal with this book is not to take sides, but rather to simply lay out the facts and then allow the reader to make their own judgments as to the people involved and the events that took place in the spring and summer of 1972, on the battleground that was the Harrisonville Square.

The Hippie Movement in America

The Hippie Movement in America did not begin in America. Instead, the American Hippie Movement was a result of Americans, mostly young people, taking an interest in other cultures, particularly those coming from the Far East. When we think of hippies today, we think of long hair, heavy drug use, sexual promiscuity, loud music, and often torn or dirty clothing choices. While those stereotypes are largely correct, there was much more that went into the Hippie Movement in America in the late 1960s and 1970s.

You can go just about as far back in time as you care to research and find examples of "hippie" behavior. In 6 BCE, there was a group that followed a school of thought in India known as the Charvaka. This group did not believe in organized religion and basically felt that people should be nice and take care of one another. In addition, they should have a great time in their life before arriving at the end of that life. They did not believe in the status quo and questioned authority and tradition whenever they could. Sound familiar? Other similar thinking groups dot the historical landscape of the far east.

In 1625, American colonists founded the colony of Merrymount in Quincy, Massachusetts. These settlers were tired of the Puritans who had come to America to escape persecution only to become the persecutors in the new society in America. (Calcagni,2) The founders of the Merrymount movement acted in ways that must have driven the Puritans crazy. They enjoyed music and dance, and erected Maypoles, which were considered a Pagan ritual by the "righteous" of the time, in their town squares.

There are several groups across the world whose beliefs and actions could be linked to what we think of as hippie culture. Further digging into the origins of the hippie culture takes the researcher back through history where they will continue to uncover societies and cultures that all had their own versions of "hippies".

What we think of as modern-day American hippies were influenced greatly by the Beat Generation, made up of a group of American writers who rose to prominence after World War II. Jack Kerouac, Allen Ginsberg, William S. Burroughs, and others were the unofficial leaders of this Beat Generation. These "Beatniks" encouraged young people to question authority and engage in drug use and sexual experimentation. They also rejected materialism, racism, and sexism, which often led to exploring alternative religious beliefs. (Calcagni,1)

Most of the young people who embraced this new Beat Generation were on the east coast but then moved to California to start what was called the San Francisco Renaissance. San Francisco became the epicenter of Hippie Culture in the United States with a large number of young people migrating to the city to join in the movement happening there. The Renaissance was thought to be an awakening of art, music, literature, thought, and religion. Participants in the Renaissance movement took much of their direction from religions with origins in Asia. (Calcagni,1) These people did not call themselves "hippies". Rather, they wanted to be known as the "beautiful people". These beautiful people were "hip" which would eventually lead to the term "hippies."

It was after World War II that drugs became a recreational activity. Before and during the war it was not uncommon for doctors to prescribe medicines that would alter a patient's state of mind. Pharmacological science was evolving, and that evolution led to some positive discoveries and some negative ones. Many of the drugs that are illegal today, were created in the hopes that they could cure illnesses. LSD was invented in the 1930's and was thought, at the time, to cure psychosis. Psychedelics, like LSD, were handed out like candy by

Figure 1: A protester at the "Love Pageant Rally" held in San Francisco on October 6, 1966.

doctors with free samples being given to many patients.

Fast forward to 1964 and the problems with many hallucinogens (like LSD) were becoming known and the government tried to step in and make sure that people were not harmed by these drugs. The hippies were not pleased. LSD, which was widely used in the hippie community, was made illegal in 1966. This government action triggered a group of hippies to organize the Love Pageant Rally, in the Haight-Ashbury district in San Francisco. An estimated twenty thousand hippies attended the rally.

While the "Love Pageant Rally" did not have the desired outcome of getting the government to reverse the ban on LSD, it did have a dramatic impact on the hippie culture and lifestyle. This was the first large-scale rally for the hippies and would lay the groundwork for many more to come over the next decade. The media coverage was substantial and acted like hippie catnip in that it attracted large numbers of young people from across America to come to California where they would be in the heart of the action in San Francisco.

Figure 2: Flyer for the "Human Be In Rally" which took place on January 14, 1967, at Golden Gate Park in San Francisco. (Content is available under Creative Commons Attribution-Noncommercial-Share Alike 3.0. • Powered by Media Wiki MediaWiki)

Another San Francisco, pro-LSD rally was planned in January of 1967, when the "Human Be-In Rally" was held in Golden Gate Park on January 14th. The rally, which attracted an estimated twenty thousand attendees, again failed to get the ban on LSD repealed, but the rally and press around it fanned the flames of the hippie fever that was spreading like wildfire across the country.

These two rallies and their attraction to the young people of the era led to a massive influx of hippies to San Francisco and what would go down in history as the "Summer of Love". During this "Summer of Love" in 1967, over 100,000 people flocked to San Francisco. The movement was migrating across the country with many young people joining and beginning to congregate in other large cities. At this point, the "hippie message" was clear. They were interested in Peace, Love, the Environment, and the Beyond. (Calcagni,3)

In the late 1960s and early 1970s, the hippies "found their voice" and that voice was the power they had by organizing and participating in protests. They protested the war in Vietnam, nuclear weapons, American military action anywhere in the world, police actions, the draft, perceived anti-environment projects, racism, and sexism, etc., etc., etc. They believed that sexual norms should be thrown out the window and behaved in ways, sexually, that shocked most conservative Americans. Hippies believed that sex was not something that should be only done or spoken about behind closed doors. Believing in the concept of "free love", they were open about sex and felt that multiple partners, one or many at a time, were perfectly acceptable. This belief did not conform to accepted societal beliefs about sex at the time.

Since thumbing their noses at tradition and societal norms was one of the primary things that drove the hippie culture, they purposely did things that violated the norms with the sole purpose of shocking and angering community leaders. This included dressing in strange clothing highlighted by strange styles, colors, and fabrics. Personal hygiene was not of great concern to the hippies. Both men and women let their hair grow, regardless of where it grew. Regular grooming was not a high priority and polite society often saw these young people as dirty and disgusting due to their lack of attention to basic hygiene. To say the least, these practices concerned and frightened conservative American society.

It was in the wake of the large protest events that the movement began to take a darker turn. Protests inevitably led to confrontations with the local police. Eventually, the police, or "pigs", along with all other authority groups became the enemy. This darker, more violent version of the hippies was led by figures such as Abbie Hoffman and Jerry Rubin. Hoffman and Rubin and some other friends started the "yippies". Yippie was the name they gave their new organization which stood for "Youth International Party". The yippies, formed in 1967 in the New York apartment of Abbie and Anita Hoffman, did not start out as a violent group. Rather, it started as a parody political party that focused on making fun of the establishment in very public ways.   The yippies would pull "street pranks" or stunts to embarrass the national leaders of the day.   Registering an actual pig for president and throwing money, some fake and some real, on the floor of the New York Stock Exchange were a couple of the pranks for which the "yippies" were well known.

Figure 3:   Top Jane Fonda and Abbie Hoffman. (CC BY 2.0.) Left Bottom: Jerry Rubin. Bottom Right: Symbol of the YIP (Youth International Party) (By Raymond1922A- own work, CC BY-SA3.0.)

The signature event in the history of the Yippies was their activity at the 1968 Democratic Convention in Chicago. In addition to nominating "Lyndon Pigasus Pig" for president, the Yippies vowed to make their presence known in Chicago at the time of the convention. The group scheduled protests, concerts, and gatherings in the same area the convention was taking place. Eventually, this led to riots where police reportedly attacked protestors and other persons who were in the area. Several bystanders, including some members of the news media, were injured during the police's attempt to control the crowd. These "injured" reporters gave the hippies a sympathetic ear in the mainstream media. By the end of the convention, several yippies were arrested, including Rubin and Hoffman.

These two men, along with five others, would stand trial in 1969 at what is now known as the "Trial of the Chicago 7". At this trial,

Hoffman and Rubin and the other defendants would rack up over 159 counts of "contempt of court" charges. The contempt citations ranged from general unruliness to showing up to court dressed as judges or colonial soldiers. Most of the contempt charges were later thrown out on appeal. Five of the seven defendants in the trial were found guilty and sentenced to five years in prison. Eighteen months later, in November of 1972, all of the convictions were reversed on appeal. None of the seven defendants would ever serve any time for their actions in Chicago during the convention.

Music and the hippie culture went hand in hand and in August of 1969 on a farm in Bethel, New York, over 500,000 hippies gathered for the "greatest of all music events" called The Woodstock Music and Art Festival. This event, which included most of the popular counter-culture musical acts of the day, would go down in history as a shining example of the hippie lifestyle and temperament. Attendees worked together and got along for three days of music in weather conditions that caused rainy weather conditions that caused the entire area and attendees to be covered in mud.

Abbie Hoffman tried to inject some politics into

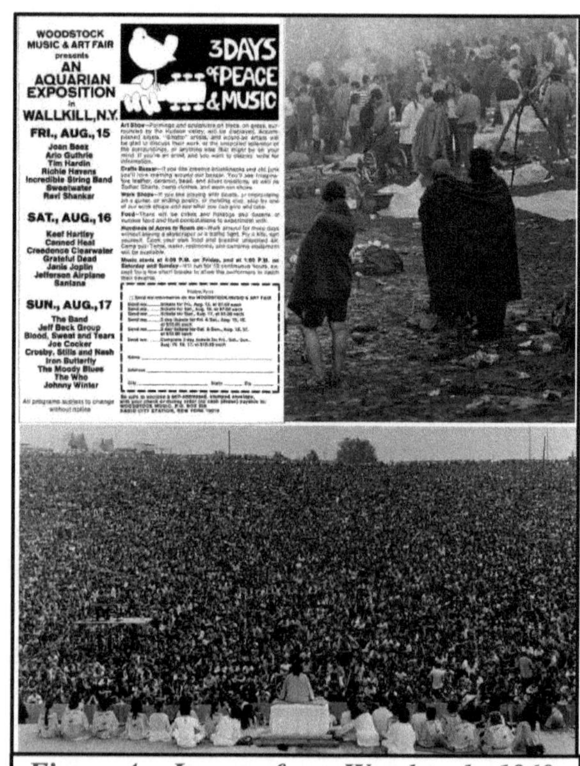

Figure 4: Images from Woodstock, 1969. Top right and bottom images are courtesy of Mark Goff. All three images are in the public domain.

Woodstock when he climbed up on the stage and grabbed the microphone while the rock band, The WHO was playing. As the band finished playing "Pinball Wizard", Hoffman jumped on stage, grabbed guitarist Pete Townshend's microphone, and shouted, "I think this is a pile of shit while John Sinclair rots in prison!" (Sinclair was a hippie poet who had been sentenced to 10 years for possession of marijuana.) Townsend, apparently not happy with Hoffman's presence on the stage, took his guitar and aggressively jabbed Hoffman in the back of the head forcing him off the stage. The crowd cheered wildly.

Showing that a massive crowd of hippies could gather together with no negative incidents was a big win for the counterculture crowd.   This hippie success story was important because only a few days before in Los Angeles, California, Charles Manson and his "family" of hippies had murdered nine people in a crime that would shock the world. Manson and his followers gave the hippie community a black mark that would be hard to escape. This black mark would follow the hippies, even though Manson was certainly not following the beliefs and ideas of the hippie movement when his followers coldly murdered their victims in Los Angeles.

A violent confrontation between

MANSON, Charles Milles

CII 966 856

Figure 5:   Charles Manson mugshot, 1969 (Photo San Quentin   Prison/Wikimedia Commons/Fair Use)

Figure 6:   Iconic image of a protester grieving a fellow protester who was shot during the Kent State incident on May 4, 1970.

the   hippies   and   authorities occurred in May of 1970, on the campus of Kent State University, during a protest of the Mai Lai Massacre   in   Vietnam   by American soldiers. At Kent State, the Ohio National Guard had been called in to help keep the peace at several days of student protests. Protesting students were said to have been pelting the National Guard soldiers with rocks and other items while the soldiers stood in formation. Eventually, shots were fired.   There is controversy as to how and why the actual shooting began, but in the end, the troops killed four and wounded nine protestors.

The positive and peaceful impression of the culture took another hit four months later in December of 1970 when the Altamont Music

Figure 7: Altamont, California. Site of "The Free Concert" at Altamont Raceway.

Festival was held in Altamont, California, a small town about 30 miles east of San Francisco. Security for the event was provided by the Hell's Angels Motorcycle Club. What could go wrong? Approximately 300,000 attendees were treated to another star-studded concert headlined by the Rolling Stones. Unfortunately, in Altamont, an 18-year-old attendee was murdered by one of the Hell's Angels providing security. Four other attendees also died of accidents at the event.

Abbie Hoffman, who had been very active during this period would go on to write a book which was published in 1971, called ***Steal this Book***. The title says it all. In his speeches, Hoffman would encourage young people to steal the book. For this reason, many bookstores would not carry the book due to the large numbers of copies being stolen. Despite this poor marketing plan, the book would sell over a quarter of a million copies. The book is still available and can be downloaded for free from various internet sites.

Steal this Book was kind of a self-help and travel guide to hippies in the early 1970s. The book contained guidelines meant to assist those without a job to get free stuff that would allow them to live the hippie lifestyle. The first part of the book is made up of chapters on how to get free food, clothing, medical treatment, legal advice, transportation, money (welfare), and drugs among other things. The book then goes into slightly more nefarious topics such as how to steal, how to fight the government, techniques of street fighting using various weapons, making bombs, and forging legal papers. Based on the contents of this book, it's not difficult to see why the "establishment" was not a big fan of Hoffman.

Figure 8: Cover of Abbie Hoffman's 1971 book, "Steal this Book", which sold over 250,000 copies.

Of course, there is much more history that goes along with the hippie movement of the 1960s and early 1970s. This very brief and high-level history is meant to give the reader an idea of what was happening in the minds and the world of young people at the time of the events on the Harrisonville Square. Leaders such as Hoffman and Rubin were among the national figures that the young people in Harrisonville looked up to at the time. In fact, the day before Charlie Simpson killed four on the Harrisonville Square, he was preparing to make copies of one of Hoffman's speeches to pass around at a protest on the square. Those copies would never be made, and the protest would never happen. Simpson decided upon a different and much more deadly course of action.

There are several names that have been used for the hippies: long-hairs, counterculture, yippies, flower children, non-conformist, and freaks, among others. Rather than trying to bounce back and forth between the names, the moniker "hippie" will be predominantly used to describe the group of young people who occupied the Harrisonville Square in the spring of 1972.

History of Cass County and Harrisonville, Missouri

In 1972, Harrisonville, Missouri, was a growing town about 30 miles south of Kansas City, with a population of just under 5,000 residents. (Census, 27) The sleepy, commuter town had experienced significant growth over the previous ten years with a growth rate of over 40%.   Town leaders expected more explosive growth with the construction of a new four-lane highway to Kansas City (Highway 71, now Interstate 49).   The new highway would make Harrisonville an even more desirable community with a quiet, small-town feel, but with easy access to the highway for workers to commute to Kansas City.

Figure 9: Present-day map of Harrisonville, MO

The town was not then and is still not today a racially diverse community.   African Americans make up only about 1% of the population. The town and its immediate surrounding area were mainly split between residents who; farmed, commuted to jobs in Kansas City, worked in local white-collar jobs, or worked in the Anaconda Wire and Cable plant located just west of town.

Harrisonville was founded in 1837 in what, at the time, was Van Buren County, which was named after President Martin Van Buren, who served as president from 1837-1841. Until 1849, Van Buren County comprised the area that is now Cass and Bates counties. In that year, the county was split, and the two new counties were formed with neither wanting to maintain the Van Buren name. Van Buren was not popular in the area as his political views had shifted over time to a pro-abolitionist viewpoint.

Cass County was named after Senator Lewis Cass who was a two-time cabinet member and presidential candidate in 1898. Lewis, a slaveholder, was a leader in The Doctrine of Popular Sovereignty, which was a belief that each state should be allowed to choose whether to allow slavery. The county was mainly settled by migrants from the surrounding states to the east of Missouri, looking for opportunities and a fresh start "out west". Harrisonville was named after Congressman Albert G. Harrison, who played a large part in securing the land on which the Harrisonville Courthouse is located.

During the Civil War, Harrisonville played a central role in the Kansas/Missouri border war, which pitted southern-leaning Missouri Bushwhackers led by men

Figure 10: Lewis Cass, Michigan Senator and namesake of Cass County, Missouri. Cass served on the cabinets of Presidents Jackson and Buchanan, as well as Governor of Michigan, and presidential candidate in 1848.

such as William Quantrill against pro-Union Kansas Jayhawkers led by the likes of Senator and General James Lane. The city was one of the few cities that was allowed to remain in existence under Order Number 11, which in 1863, decreed that parts of Jackson County, and all of Cass and Bates Counties would be evacuated to stop pro-confederate residents from supporting the local leaning bushwhackers, sometimes called guerillas. In Cass County, only Harrisonville and Pleasant Hill were allowed to remain in existence as Union military posts. Citizens in the county were allowed to remain in those towns as long as they took an oath to support the Union cause.

After the war, Union leadership in Kansas City made it difficult for many of the pro-southern residents of Cass County to come back to their homes by requiring full payment of back taxes. Many of these returning residents did not have the money to pay the back taxes and thus lost their homes to the tax collectors. Only about 30% of the residents of Cass County who were left homeless by Order Number 11 were able to come back and reclaim their property after the war. This allowed for rampant land speculation by pro-union men and a dramatic shift in the political leanings of the citizenry. The speculators made sure to only sell the properties to the "right kind" of people, aka, people who agreed with their political ideology.

This political shift was short-lived and today the county is predominantly conservative. The last democratic presidential candidate to carry the county was Jimmy Carter in 1976. Today, Harrisonville is a strongly conservative, predominantly Caucasian, small town in the middle of the mostly conservative state of Missouri. Politically, Cass County leans right and joins most all other rural counties in the state in that view.

Harrisonville, 1972

I grew up in Harrisonville, Missouri. In my mind, Harrisonville was no different than the town of Mayberry that we watched in black and white on the Andy Griffith Show on televisions that only got three channels. I realize that my middle-class parents, like many Harrisonville parents, sheltered my siblings and me from anything that would destroy that Mayberry notion and the feeling of safety that came with it. During my childhood and adolescence, I don't remember anything bad happening in Harrisonville. It was just a small town in rural Missouri, just like thousands of other Missouri small towns.

Figure 11: Image from a Harrisonville postcard. Likely taken in the 1960s.

In Harrisonville in the 1970s, children would leave the house in the morning with the instruction to "be home before dark". Meals would be eaten at whichever friend's house you found yourself when lunchtime came around. Most parents never gave a thought of anything bad happening to their children as they roamed the town unsupervised. It was quite normal to see kids riding bikes to the store, to baseball practice, or to visit the soda fountain at one of the drugstores located on the historic Harrisonville Square.

Teenagers with cars would "cruise the circuit" before ending up on the square later in the evening as that is the one place where everyone could park and talk to their friends. Friday nights in the fall would include going to the Wildcat football games and then heading out to a party or simply cruising the circuit hoping to find friends or to make new ones. Like every other small town in America before and after 1972, kids complained that there was nothing to do in town and the only way to have any fun was to either go to Kansas City or find a party to attend. Harrisonville, the largest town in southern Cass County, was a destination for young people from the many small towns in the surrounding areas. Teenagers from Archie, East Lynn, Freeman, Garden City, Pleasant Hill, Adrian, Lone Jack, and others would travel to Harrisonville on Friday and Saturday nights to join others their age who were congregating in town.

Race relations in Harrisonville were the same as they were in many small towns all over the midwest. African Americans were confined to the balcony in the Lee Theater and the thought of their daughters dating a black man brought rage to the minds of many Harrisonville fathers. Today, most Americans would cringe when hearing some of the quotes about race that were recorded in the press in 1972. A Harrisonville merchant who was driving a reporter around town to show him where some of the hippies had lived, had this to say about the black community, "The house was in what we used to call 'Nig***town', but you can see our Negroes are good people. We haven't been bothered by any from the outside." Police Chief Davis had this to say about his black neighbors, "We've got about 50 blacks in town, all good people who have been here pretty much all their lives. Some are pretty damn good friends of mine." (Wilks, 1)

The Kansas City Star writer, Harry Jones Jr., in his article after the shooting, writes that a "phenomenon" was taking place in Harrisonville in late 1971 and early 1972. Jones contends that many of Harrisonville's own were coming back from either college or the military. Many of these young people were returning with a whole new set of ideas and a new lifestyle, neither of which matched up with the ideas of their parents or local civic leaders. (Jones, Portrait)

In 1972, the Harrisonville Square was the center point for most of the business conducted in the town. The diagram below shows the businesses on the square in 1972. The second image shows, via color codes, the types of businesses that occupied the square at this time.

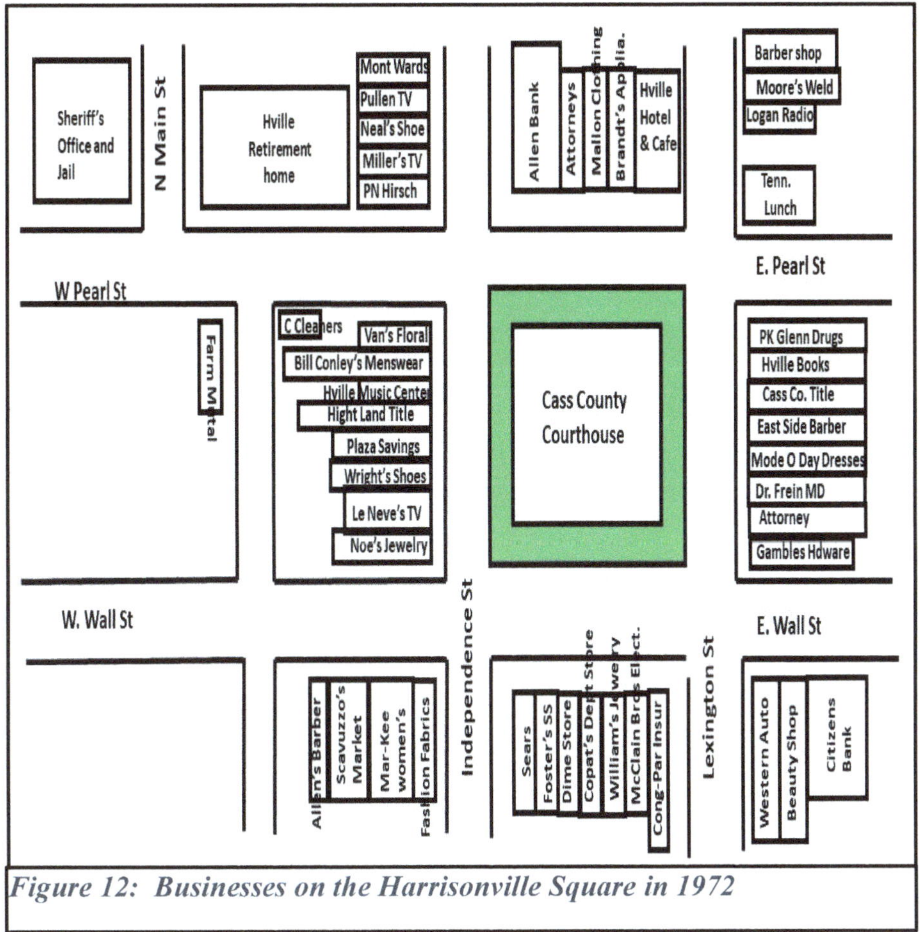

Figure 12: Businesses on the Harrisonville Square in 1972

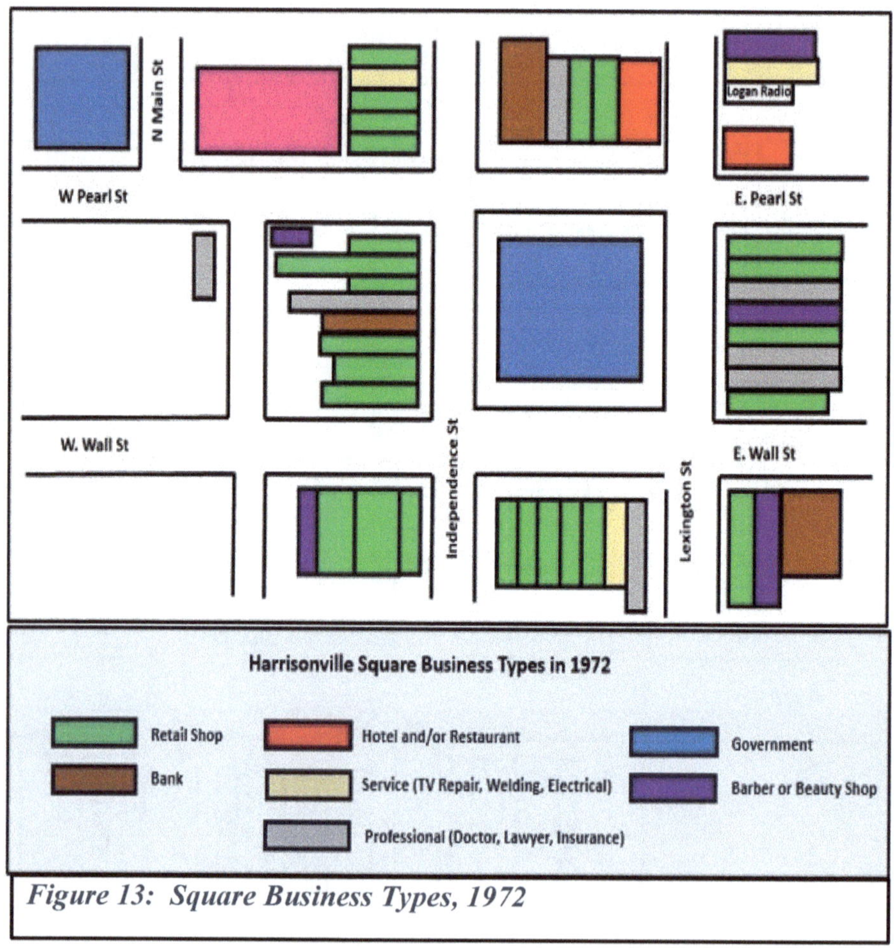

Figure 13: Square Business Types, 1972

As can be seen clearly in Figure 14 at this time the square was full of customer-oriented operations. Significant foot traffic was critical as over 50% of the businesses on the square in 1972 were retail operations including men's and women's clothing stores, shoe stores, and TV and appliance stores. There were only a few professional offices, attorneys, doctors, and title companies on the square at the time which meant that the majority of the other businesses that were not retail, were service-related merchants including barbers, beauty shops, shoe repair, tv repair, cleaners, and banks. These service businesses also relied on and generated significant foot traffic. The desire and need for foot traffic meant that anything that kept customers away from the square was bad for business.

In the spring of 1972, a group of hippies started hanging out on the square which was deemed "bad for business". Something had to be done. But what?

Team Harrisonville

The problem of what to do about the hippies fell squarely on the shoulders of the town's elected and non-elected leaders. This chapter will identify the key people who represented the town in various ways in the interaction with the young hippies who, in the opinion of the square merchants, were driving business away from the square. Other persons became involved in the story who will be introduced later. The people introduced in this chapter were involved in the beginning and initially tasked with solving the "hippie problem". In some cases, the best I can do is relate to the reader the title of the person, as in some cases there is very little information about an individual. In other cases, I can present a clear picture of the person, their role, and status in Harrisonville at the time.

Mayor M.O. Raine

In the spring of 1972, Mayor M.O. Raine was celebrating being elected for his second, 2-year term, as mayor of Harrisonville. Mayor Raine was a 73-year-old, local dentist who had spent 35 years practicing dentistry from an office in the hotel building on the northwest corner of the square. Mayor Raine had graduated from Kansas City-Western Dental College and then worked as a Food and Drug Administrator before starting his dental career with stops in Downing and Saint Joseph, Missouri.

Raine had big plans for Harrisonville and felt that the city was on the cusp of exponential growth mainly due to its location and the prospect of a new four-lane highway.

Figure 14:   Figure 15: Harrisonville Mayor M.O. Raine (Photo Courtesy of Tim Raine)

We're just an overgrown small town, but we've got growing pains. There's a lot of people wanting to get out of Kansas City who are looking at us because we are a small community near the city. We're sitting here on Highway 71 and Highway 291.... we're dealing with other companies now, trying to get them to locate here. We're not going to give out any names for fear we would run them off. But Harrisonville is going places. (Hood)

It's fair to say that the situation on the square was not helping the mayor in his goal to attract more businesses and citizens to his town.

G.M. Allen

G.M. Allen was the Harrisonville Fire Chief and local leader of The Civil Defense organization. Allen, who was 58 in 1972, was one of the "city leaders" who seemed to antagonize the hippies the most.   Allen's strong criticism and calls for action against the hippies are the reason that the tension with the square hippies is sometimes called "Allen's War".

G.M. (George Monroe) Allen graduated from Harrisonville High School in 1932 and was named to the school's "Wall of Fame" in 2006. Allen was a World War II Veteran serving in the 13th Armored Division

Figure 15: Figure 16: 1972 Harrisonville fire chief, G.M. Allen

where he earned the Bronze Star for Valor. Allen spent most of his professional life in the banking business where he served as the president of Harrisonville's Citizens Bank for 21 years. It is this job at the bank, located on East Wall Street just off the square, that allowed him to witness the situation with the hippies on the square on a daily basis.

It would be fair to call G.M. Allen, "Mr. Harrisonville" during this time. He is a man that spent his entire life serving Harrisonville in a wide variety of civic roles, including, volunteer fire chief, school board member, commander of both the local VFW and American Legions posts, member of the Masonic Lodge, president of Kiwanis Club,

Harrisonville Civic Association, Chamber of Commerce, and chairman of the local chapters of the American Red Cross and March of Dimes.

Allen would later serve for 10 years as a state representative for the local district from 1976-1986. *The Belton Star Herald* described Allen in this way,

His low-key style, coupled with his interest in issues which affected all areas of his legislative district, earned him a reputation for fairness and effectiveness with voters of various political persuasions. (G.M. Allen, 1)

G.M. Allen was a man who was used to getting his way when it came to Harrisonville issues.

Harrisonville City Council

The Harrisonville City Council was made up of eight elected members, two from each of four city "wards". Council members were elected to 2-year terms, with one of the members from each ward up for election each April.   The chart below shows the members of the City Council between 1970 and 1972.

		Northeast	Northwest	Southwest	Southeast
1970		CA Jones	Robert Noe	Dr George Freeman	Robert Beckerdite
		Luke Scavuzzo	Bill Plattner	FJ Thomas	John D. Allen
1971		Ted Behler	Robert Noe	Felix Hacker	VF Lafoon
		Luke Scavuzzo	Bill Plattner	FJ Thomas	John D. Allen
1972		Ted Behler	Harold Friederich	Felix Hacker	VF Lafoon
		Luke Scavuzzo	CB Price	FJ Thomas	John D. Allen

Figure 16: Members of the Harrisonville City Council between 1970 and 1972.

In the interest of full disclosure, you will note that the representative for the Northeast Ward in 1970 is C.A. Jones, my late father. My dad passed away in 2019. He and I never spoke about the events on the square in 1972. To be honest, I didn't even realize his involvement with the council until I started researching this book and realized that he was on the council around this time. His term expired in April of 1971, before most of the events on the square occurred.   He was a great man who served the city of Harrisonville for many years starting on the City Council, then the school board, and finally serving three terms as mayor.

That said, his position and history has not influenced how this story is being told.

Sheriff Bill Gough

Bill Gough was the Cass County Sheriff in 1972. He was 46 years old. Gough was elected to the position in 1968 beginning his first of four terms as sheriff in 1969. Gough, his wife Betty Lou, and their son, Ron, lived in the front portion of the jail building in 1972.

Bill E. Gough graduated from Garden City High School and then joined the Army Air Corps with whom he would serve three years during World War II. Upon returning from his tour in the service, he managed a building supply store and later worked as a machine maintenance mechanic for Hallmark and Western Electric.

Sheriff Gough would go on to serve 16 years as the Cass County Sheriff from 1969 through 1985. After his tenure as the sheriff, he would serve as a Cass County Commissioner as well as police chief of Archie, Missouri.

Figure 17:   Cass County Sheriff Bill E. Gough (Image Courtesy of Ron Gough)

Police Chief Bill Davis

Harrisonville Chief of Police, William Davis, was a Harrisonville native having grown up in a home that is now part of the property occupied by the Harrisonville Community Center. Davis served as a police captain in Harrisonville. The role of police captain was very similar to that of police chief. In the late 1960s, the city changed its organizational structure and William Davis' title changed from police captain to police chief. Chief Davis retired from his position around 1986.

Figure18: 1972 Harrisonville Police Chief, William Davis

Everett Wade, Juvenile Officer

Everett Wade, referred to by Eszterhas as "turtle-headed", was the Cass County Juvenile officer in 1972. He had held that position for 14 years at the time of the events on the square. Wade's office was in the courthouse with a window overlooking the spot where the hippies congregated. He had been tasked with watching the hippies and recording anything that he saw from his office window.

Everett Wade had been an industrial arts teacher in the Harrisonville schools before joining the Army during World War II. After returning from the war, he worked with the Veterans Administration before taking the job as the Juvenile officer with the 17th Judicial Circuit in Harrisonville. Wade would retire in 1976 and pass away two years later in 1978 at the age of 66. Cass County's Everett E. Wade Juvenile Center bears his name.

Don F. Whitcraft, Cass County Prosecutor

Don Whitcraft was the Cass County Prosecutor in 1972. Before being elected to that office, Whitcraft was a Harrisonville attorney practicing law out of an office at 103 E Wall St on the Harrisonville Square. In his private practice, Whitcraft seemed to focus on family law handling divorces and estates. Whitcraft becomes a more important player in the story after the shooting.

Whitcraft was elected to his office in November 1962 and took office in January 1963. He would serve as Cass County Prosecutor until he was elected Magistrate Judge, taking office in January of 1975. In his early years as a judge, Whitcraft engaged in conflict with his fellow Cass County judges in a dispute over unauthorized expenditures. After suffering a heart attack, Whitcraft lost his

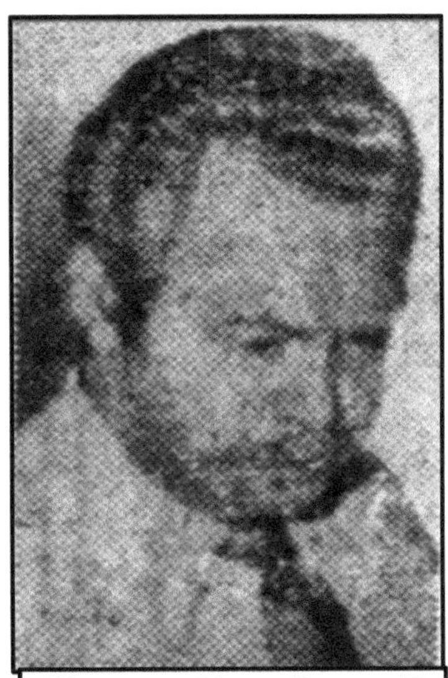

Figure 19: Don F. Whitcraft, Cass County 1972 Prosecuting Attorney

bid for re-election in 1982 ending his tenure as an Associate Circuit Judge after three terms.

Sergeant James Harris

Sergeant Jim Harris was 46 years old in 1972. A Navy Veteran, Harris served as a police officer in Rich Hill and Butler, Missouri. Shortly after the events on the Harrisonville Square, Harris would join Sheriff Bill Gough and work as a deputy for the Cass County Sheriff's Department.   In 1972, Harris held the rank of sergeant in the Harrisonville Police Department and was heavily involved in the hippie conflict.

A couple of the people that I interviewed described Harris as a person you tried to avoid. One described him this way, "He was just mean. Like a dog with a bone when he got after something." Another described him simply as "a jerk". When told of these quotes about Sergeant Harris, a person that worked with him in law enforcement commented, "I can see that." They went on to describe Harris as a guy who "if he liked you, he would do anything for you. If he didn't, he would be your worst nightmare."

Charles R. Simpson

Charles Richard Simpson was born on March 7, 1947, to Charles (Ike) Burnis Simpson and Helen Louis (Loveall) Simpson in rural Missouri. The elder Simpson was a World War II Veteran who was injured in the war and lived out the rest of his life in very poor health and on disability. His son Charles Richard was the firstborn to the rural Missouri couple and would be followed by a brother, Elwyn (Bub) two years later, and a sister Marlah, five years after that. During most of their childhood, the family would live in a small house just outside of Urich.

Figure 19: Charlie's father, Charles (Ike) Burnis Simpson. Ike was 53 years old in 1972.

Charlie's cousin, Rita Simpson Inman, relates that even though Charlie's father, Ike Simpson, had one brother and three sisters, the family was not close and despite close proximity geographically, the only time they gathered as an extended family seemed to be for funerals. Rita remembers Ike as a very frail old man, who never worked outside of the home due to his health issues. Rita recalls Charlie's mother, Helen, as a woman who was slightly detached from happenings around her, but with a bad temper. In fact, a bad temper seemed to be one of the traits that flowed through this branch of the Simpson clan.

Charles began to suffer from asthma around the age of 7, but the breathing disorder didn't seem to slow him down as his friends remember him running with them in hayfields and being able to "keep up just fine". Asthma would eventually keep Charlie from enlisting in the military.

Figure 20: Charles R. Simpson. Image was likely taken in 1962, during his freshman year in high school. There are very few photos of Charlie Simpson in existence.

When Charlie was a teenager, the family still lived in the small house just off Route B, north of Urich. Charlie attended Sherwood High School, which is located just outside of the small town of Creighton, Missouri. In 1970, Creighton boasted a population of 294 residents. Sherwood High School was, and still is, a regional school that serves a largely agricultural population, drawing students from the small towns of Garden City, Blairstown, Urich, and Hartwell. Even though Charlie was an average to a poor student, he did get within 1 ½ credits of graduating, but instead decided to leave school his senior year, 1966.

A teacher at Sherwood High School, James Adkins, remembers Simpson as "…quiet, and as a student was near average. The boy wore a crew cut. He was no problem at all." (Wilks, 1) ***Charlie Simpson's Apocalypse*** author Joe Eszterhas contradicts Adkins' memory when he claims that Charlie was a poor student largely because he would often skip school to simply lay around in the fields near his home. In his book, he relates a story about an incident between Charlie and an English teacher at the high school. According to the story, a female teacher, whom he refers to as a "bony maple-headed spinster", attempted to motivate Charlie by making fun of him, calling him a "dumb peckerwood". According to the story, Charlie did nothing at the time but later followed the teacher after school, ran full speed at her, and viciously tackled her into a ditch. He

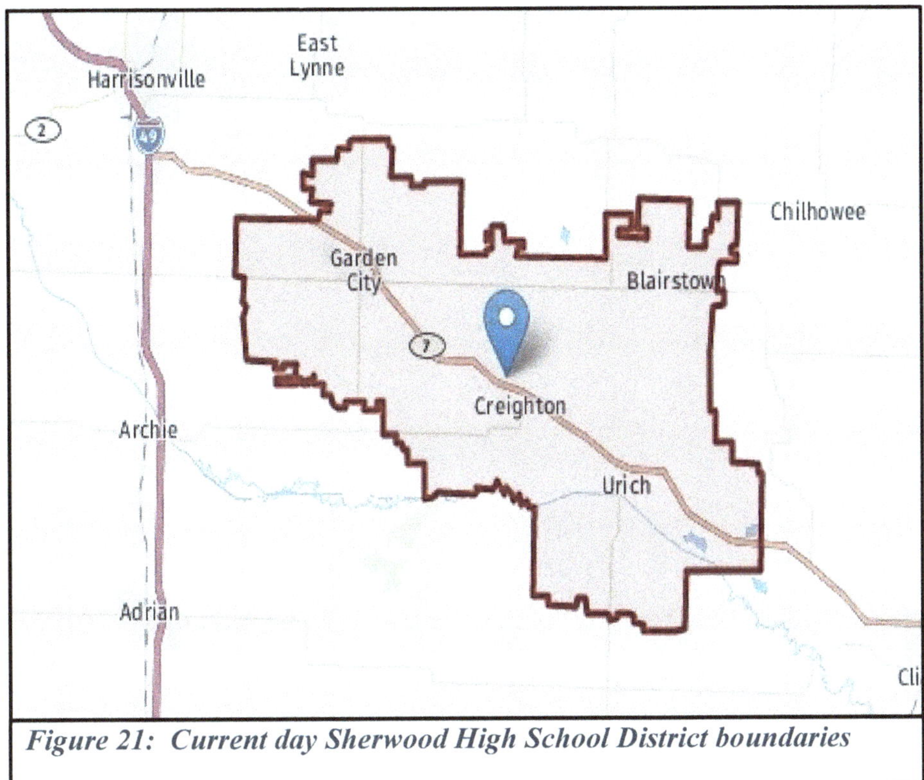

Figure 21: Current day Sherwood High School District boundaries

was understandably suspended for this act. (Eszterhas, Charlie, 68) I can find nothing to substantiate this story, and the people that I have spoken to who knew Charlie as a young man also had no recollection of this story. In a future police report, Charlie's father, Ike, mentions problems with a high school literature teacher, but says nothing about any physical altercation between the two.

It is important to note that at this point in history, it was not rare for high-school age young men to drop out of school to either go to work or enter the military. Military service was not an option for Charlie as he was designated 4-F due to his asthma. We do not know exactly why Charlie decided to drop out during his senior year, especially since he was only 1.5 credits away from graduation. Charlie's father cites a bad case of mumps his senior year as one of the reasons for Charlie's decision to drop out. In hindsight, it certainly looks like a questionable decision in a lifetime of questionable decisions for the young Charlie Simpson.

After dropping out of high school, Charlie got a job at Stahl Specialty, a foundry in Kingsville, Missouri. At Stahl, Charlie worked with his brother, Bub, and one of his best friends, Paul Smith. The three men also shared a house in Harrisonville, directly across from Harrisonville High School, now the location of Harrisonville Middle School. After several months in the house, the trio moved to an apartment on the northeast corner of Mechanic and Independence Street, above K & J Furniture.

Figure 22: The two circles in this image show the locations of places where Paul Smith, Charlie Simpson, and Bub Simpson lived in the late 1960s in Harrisonville. The apartment was above K & J Furniture. The house was located where the public library now stands.

Stahl Specialty was a foundry, or a metalworking shop, located in Kingsville, Missouri about 50 miles from Harrisonville, where the young men lived. Charlie and Bub worked together on the night shift as welders and buffers for a couple of years, probably from around 1966-1968. Eventually, Charlie missed work on a Monday and was fired for this unexcused absence when he came in to work on Tuesday. According to Eszterhas, Charlie argued that he had informed his boss that he would be out on Monday, and it was wrong to fire him for that offense. A couple of days later Charlie marched into his ex-boss's office at the foundry and demanded that if they wanted to fire him that was fine, but not for missing work as he had told the boss he was going to be gone. Eszterhas claims that the boss was frightened by this "demon-eyed raving hippie" and changed the official record. This allowed Charlie to file for unemployment, which he did a week later. (Eszterhas, Charlie, 82)

Bub and Charlie's roommate, Paul Smith, was a childhood friend of the Simpson brothers, having grown up together in the Urich area. While living in the house directly across the street from Harrisonville High school, Paul met Sharon Dicke, a high school junior, who he would marry in 1968. Sharon spent a considerable amount of time at the house and apartment where the men lived and

Figure 23: Paul Smith, 1972. (Photo courtesy of Sharon Smith)

remembers that if they weren't working, they would be laying around drinking, getting high on marijuana, or looking for a party around Harrisonville.

After his marriage, Paul stopped living with the Simpson boys and began to work the 2nd shift at the General Motors automotive factory in Kansas City. Paul joined the Marines in 1968 and lost touch with Charlie and Bub until he returned from Vietnam in 1971. Both Sharon Smith and Rita Simpson Inman remember Charlie Simpson in his late teenage years and early 20s as a happy-go-lucky guy, who would help anyone when needed. While both women lost track of Charlie after around 1968, they do not remember him being obsessed with world events or other current social issues.

Charlie and Bub would live in several locations after Paul was married. Their hobby during this time, besides smoking pot, was trying to build a race car, which they intended to race once it was running properly.   Eszterhas goes into great detail about the successes and failures that the brothers experienced during their quest to get their car ready to race. Mostly failures. The one time they got the car to the racetrack in Kansas City, it never left the starting line due to mechanical issues. The boys limped home with their broken-down car and soon gave up trying to get it race-ready. I'm assuming it is Bub who related to Eszterhas that they had spent nearly $9,000 on parts for the car. The cost was a large reason that Charlie gave up on building the car. He felt that the parts dealers "kept screwing us." (Jones, Portrait) The brothers ended up selling the car for a fraction of what they had spent.

During his late teenage years and early 20s, Charlie was known to local law enforcement, but mainly for minor transgressions. It is likely during this time that Simpson began to cultivate his disdain for law enforcement and authority. Several of Charlie's legal issues at this point either dealt with traffic violations or for displaying a lack of respect for authorities. He was known to yell and make rude gestures to local law enforcement officers, which often resulted in his being stopped or arrested. Throughout his young adult life, Charlie had spent time in many of the jails around Cass, Henry, and Johnson Counties. His friend, Avery Newman, notes that Charlie saw himself as a victim because the sons of wealthy residents of whatever small town he was in could get away with the same small offenses for which he would be ticketed or arrested. This idea of "victimhood" would become a theme in Charlie Simpson's short life.

Figure 24: Sketch of how Charlie Simpson may have looked at age 25 (Commissioned work)

By this time Charlie had physically matured into a man. He was taller than most at six foot two inches tall and muscular, but thin weighing in at around 190 pounds. He sported black hair, which was worn long, hanging down to his shoulders. He was generally clean-shaven with no mustache or beard. He was said to have been a good-looking man, not lacking female admirers. Sharon Smith remembers that Charlie had plenty of girls willing to have sex with him. Joe Eszterhas would describe Simpson as having "high jutting cheekbones, a hooked and fist-kissed nose, a swarthy complexion, and uneven calcimine white teeth." The few pictures I have seen, of which very few are available, dispute the "high cheekbones' description as his cheeks were fleshier with no visible cheekbones. The image below is a composite drawing using one of the few images of Simpson as a young man and then adding longer hair than is seen in the existing image.

From the time he dropped out of school, Charlie was regularly seen hanging around the Harrisonville Square. It is also around this time that Charlie would have met Janice Maloney. Janice was a 17-year-old, recent high school graduate from Adrian, Missouri. Adrian is a small town from which many teens made the trip to Harrisonville on weekends to hang out with more kids their age. Janice recalls that in Adrian, teenagers either chose to go to Butler or Harrisonville since those were the two largest towns nearby. Janice chose Harrisonville because she had more friends there than she did in Butler.

Janice's first memory of Charlie is when, on the square, someone said something unkind to her and Charlie went after this guy and "beat the tar out of him." She does not remember what was said and recalls that she was surprised that he defended her as they didn't even know each other at this point.

Janice is part of this story because after that first meeting, they would become friends, and eventually, she would give birth to Charlie Simpson's child in March of 1970. Janice was in a long-term relationship with a boyfriend in Harrisonville that had just recently become sexual. The weekend she was with Charlie, she was angry because her current beau had left for Vietnam a day before he told her he was leaving. She went to see him off only to find that he was already gone. This anger led to a night of revenge in Harrisonville, where, in an era of free love, she had sexual relations with Charlie Simpson, a good-looking, older man. The sexual encounter was a one-time event, but Janice and Charlie would continue to interact socially after she became pregnant. Charlie is one of the few people she had told about the pregnancy. They both assumed that the previous boyfriend was the father of the child. Janice would not learn the truth about the father of her child until 50 years later when the daughter that was given up for adoption at birth reached out to Janice, her biological mother. A DNA test would confirm for both of them that the daughter's biological father was Charlie Simpson.

After learning of her pregnancy, Janice's family shipped her off to Crittenton House, which at the time was a place where families sent young, unmarried, girls to live and work while going through an "unwanted" pregnancy. At Crittenton House, the pregnant young ladies were assigned to a family home in which they worked as nannies or housekeepers while their pregnancy progressed. Janice found that life with her assigned family was not for her and went back home to Adrian in less than 3 weeks. She would remain at home until it was time for the baby to be born, which occurred in March of 1970 at Crittenton House. The baby was immediately given up for adoption.

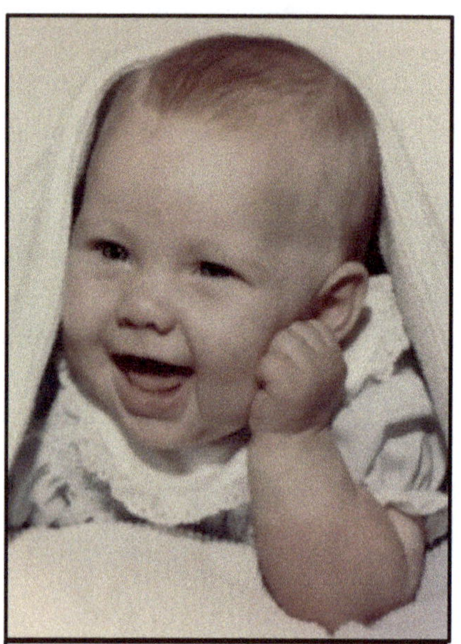

Figure 25: Infant daughter of Janice Maloney and Charlie Simpson, born March 1970. (Photo Courtesy of Kathryn Hackett)

After the birth, Janice went back to Adrian and resumed life as a young adult. She met her first husband shortly after giving birth and they were married a couple of months later in May 1970. After giving birth and then getting married, she no longer hung around with the crowd on the Harrisonville Square and lost track of most of the friends from that era in her life. She did see Charlie "around town" and they would wave at each other on these occasions.

Janice has fond memories of her time and friendships in Harrisonville, specifically her time with Charlie. She recalls going to Harrisonville to meet up with friends from different towns to hang out and sometimes party. Her memory is very clear that in the years that she frequented the Harrisonville party scene, drug use was not commonplace. She remembers that alcohol was the drug of choice for the Harrisonville teenage crowd in 1968-1969. She remembers that they would often meet on the town square, spending evenings talking and figuring out where the party, if there was one, was going to be that night. The square was a meeting point, where the kids would get together and figure out where to go next.

Janice remembers Charlie Simpson as a gentle, soft-spoken person, attractive, and a bit of a loner. During the time she was acquainted with Charlie, she did not consider him a leader, but he was someone that the younger kids looked up to due to his age, which made it easy for him to make friends. Janice remembers him as a guy who felt uncomfortable by silence and if nobody was talking, he would fill that void, just to keep the conversation going. At the time of their interactions in 1968-1969, Janice does not remember Charlie being obsessed with politics or world affairs. She remembers that he would talk about these things occasionally, but not regularly. She outwardly wonders what happened to the gentle soul that she knew in 1969 and what changed in him that led to him murdering three people in cold blood three short years later.

In the late 1960s, when Charlie was 21 years old, his mother and father separated with his mother leaving the family home. Charlie moved in with his mother for a short time until she decided to leave Missouri for California. By 1970, Bub had married, left home, and moved in with his new wife. Charlie was either not asked to accompany his mother to California or he simply decided not to go. When she moved out of state, Charlie, now 23, moved back in with his father who now lived in Holden, population 2,089.

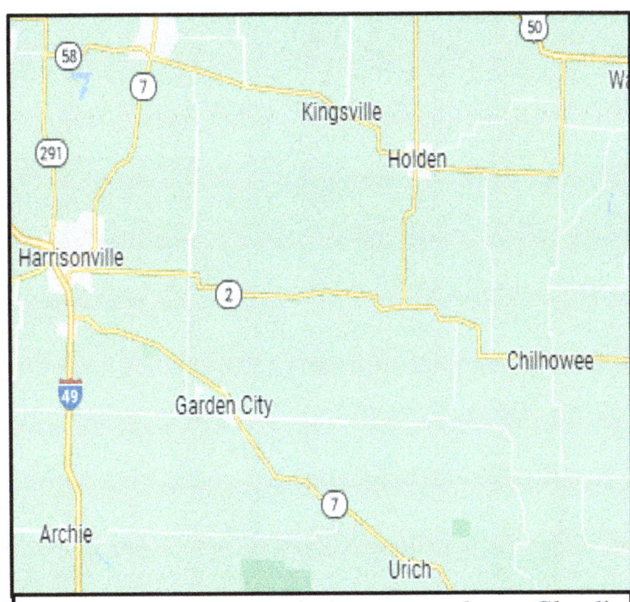

Figure 26: Map of the area where Charlie Simpson spent his time. Living in Harrisonville, Urich, and Holden, and working in Kingsville at Stahl Specialty.

It was during this time of turmoil in his personal life that Charlie began to become interested in politics. He began reading the "manifestos" of the hippie influencers of the day such as Abbie Hoffman and Henry David Thoreau. It was not uncommon to see him reading works by the revolutionary hippie leaders of the day nor thumbing through an edition of *Psychology Today* or *Guns and Ammo* magazines. His father took note of how during this time his lack of respect for authority grew almost out of control, saying. "He expressed his feelings to plain. You can't do that, especially with law officers." (Jones, Portrait)

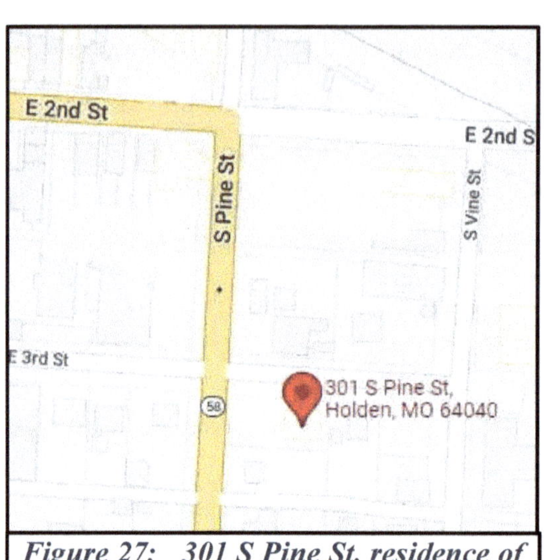

Figure 27:   301 S Pine St, residence of Ike, Bub, and Charlie Simpson in April 1972

Charlie traveled quite a bit in 1970 and 1971 attending a war demonstration in Washington D.C. and making several road trips around the country to camp and fish. When he was back in the area, Charlie, now living with his father in Holden, would often come to Harrisonville to party with the crowd on the square. At times, he would often camp near North Lake, outside of town, rather than drive back to Holden after a night of partying.

It was during these times that Charlie, now in his early 20s, began his

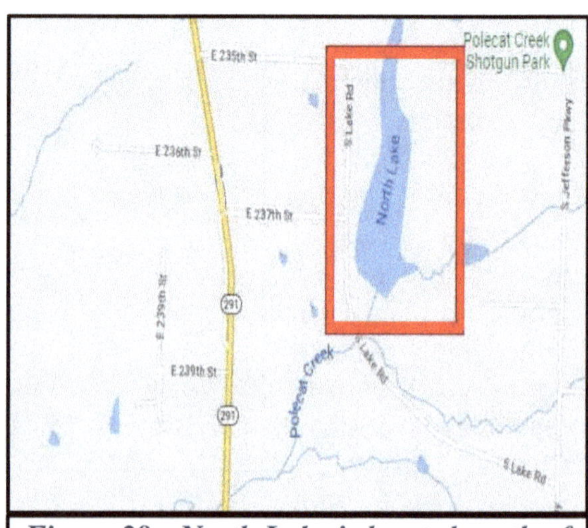

Figure 28: North Lake is located north of Harrisonville, just east of Highway 291.

intense dislike for Harrisonville authorities. He again felt that the Harrisonville authorities had one set of rules for the merchants and middle class and another for the poor and the long hairs, like he and his friends. Fellow hippie, Jim Thompson remembers, "He was poor all his life, you know? And he was down on people because of the way they treated the black and poor and Indians." (Jones, Portrait) Other sources point to the fact that Charlie had a long list of grievances with the world in general on topics including ecology, racism, sexism, problems with the police, and problems with prison reform.

It was during this time he got the nickname "Ootney" from the Harrisonville crowd. It is said that he got this nickname from an "old geezer" who owned a carryout place on Highway 7. The old man would refer to Simpson as "rootin tootin" Mr. Simpson" every time he came into the store. What began with Win Allen and John Risner calling Charlie "rootin tootin" eventually somehow morphed into "Ootney". (Eszterhas, Charlie, 98)

During his early 20s, Charlie expanded his criminal career beyond the traffic violations of his youth. Eszterhas tells many stories of arrests in several different towns across the states of Missouri and Kansas. While these offenses were more serious than his previous traffic arrests, they were still low-level crimes such as verbally assaulting a police officer, urinating in a public place, public indecency, and fleeing from a police officer.

Holden Police Chief, Albert Wakeman, described Charlie this way:

He seemed to be in with the militant people. . . He was very belligerent toward police or authority." He remembers Charlie calling him a "pig" several times, [his words] got a little stronger at times. "He believed he was always getting the short end of the stick. He always had the feeling that he was being picked on. (Harrisonville Hunts, 6)

In his book, Eszterhas bounces back and forth between these crime stories being Charlie's fault or at times the fault of his belief that he was always being picked on. The truth likely lay somewhere in between the two options. As the cops began to know Charlie better, they likely began watching him a little closer, similar to how a teacher watches a class troublemaker a little closer than they watch other students. One can only assume that calling them "fucking pigs" didn't exactly endear

Charlie to the local authorities. In a police interview, Charlie's father comments that his son saw himself as a leader of the hippie crowd in Harrisonville. Charles Sr felt that the other hippies took advantage of that belief by pushing Charlie out in front when trouble began. (Police)

In the spring of 1971, Charlie's old friend Paul Smith, having served his tour in the Marines, came home and the two renewed their friendship. Paul and Sharon Smith were living in Ruskin while Paul worked the second shift at the General Motors plant in Kansas City and Sharon worked at a warehouse store in Grandview, called GEM, located just east of 71 Highway. Charlie convinced Paul Smith to purchase an M-1 Carbine from the GEM store for him.   Charlie asked Paul to purchase the gun because due to Sharon's employment at the store, she received an employee discount on the purchase.

Once the firearm was purchased, Paul sold the gun to Charlie making sure that all legal documents were properly filled out and submitted. It seems a

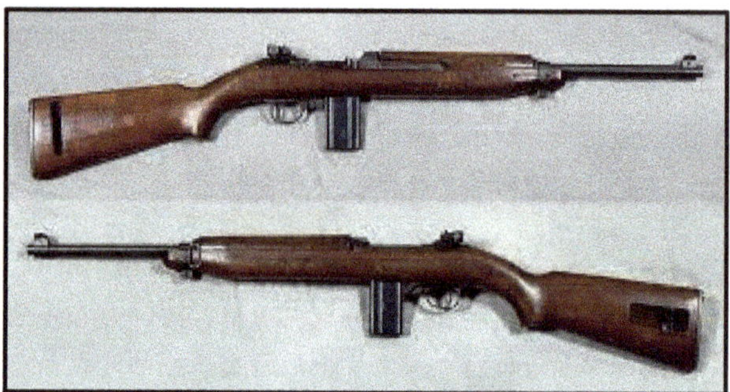

Figure 29: This image shows a 30 Caliber, M-1 Carbine like the one purchased for Charlie by Paul Smith at the GEM store in Grandview.

bit odd that Paul was such a stickler regarding the paperwork for the gun transfer. Odd, but fortunate for Paul, as the gun would later be used for a terrible purpose.   Sharon Smith recalls that at the time, her husband, Paul Smith, believed that Charlie just wanted the gun for target practice and maybe to shoot squirrels or other small animals. She remembers going, with Paul, to meet Charlie out near Holden where the men would shoot beer cans with the weapon. Did Charlie have a grand scheme to use the gun in a more nefarious way? Maybe, we will never know for sure.

The gun was an M-1 carbine, which is a lightweight, semi-automatic weapon that was a standard military weapon used in World War II, the Korean War, and the Vietnam War. The term "carbine" means that the barrel was a bit shorter than a normal rifle, which made it easier to carry and use in close combat. In the 1960s and 1970s, the weapon became popular with police forces around the world as well as a popular choice for civilians. The weapon had a standard clip that allowed the user to shoot 15 rounds per clip. The term "semi-automatic" means that the user had to pull the trigger for each shot, unlike an automatic where the user could just hold down the trigger and spray bullets.

By 1971, Charlie Simpson was evolving into a leader to the young people that congregated on the Harrisonville Square. About to turn 25, Charlie's world experiences had turned him into the "go-to" person to speak with regarding how the world was "going to hell". Charlie would tell these young people that the only way to bring about change was through revolution. He was said to lead discussions or give sermons on the issues of the day. According to John Risner, he would sometimes take both sides of an issue only to later claim loudly that "he never said any of that shit". Risner said that the gang began to call these flip-flops one of "Ootney's Acts". (Eszterhas, Charlie, 98)

Each person I spoke with that knew Charlie Simpson personally called him a "gentle soul". In these interviews, he was generally described as a soft-spoken, caring, and generally nice guy. While some of the other hippies in the group were quick to respond in a physical way to confrontation and criticism, Charlie would typically respond by making a verbal argument with the opposing party. Acquaintances say that these arguments were well worded and intelligently laid out in hopes that the other party might understand his point of view.

Team Hippie

The group of hippies that congregated on the square in 1972 was comprised of both men and women. It is mentioned in the accounts from the day that some females, as young as 14-years-old were part of the crowd. In newspapers the size of the hippie crowd on the square ranged from 30 up to as many as 100. Accounts from eyewitnesses to whom I have spoken, lead me to believe it was usually more like 10 – 20 regulars in the group. Many of the young people were still in high school. When asked what attracted the high schoolers, 'teeny bros' according to Eszterhas, John Risner proclaimed,

We told the kids the truth. They'd come to us about the dress code at the high school, for instance, and we'd tell them, 'Stand up for your rights'. When they wanted truth about things, they'd come to us instead of their teachers. (Jones, Vigilantes, 1)

This book concentrates on the male hippies simply because very few of the females are mentioned anywhere in the public records. In this chapter I have listed the members of the group who are either named in press clippings from 1972 or named in court or police records from that year. This "group of hippies" ranged from a 26-year-old military Veteran to high school seniors who would have been 17 or 18 at the time. Some of the younger members had older brothers who were also part of the group. The Thompson family had three brothers in the group, Jim (26), John (22) and Romie (18), while Gary (24) and Steve Hale (17) represented the Hale family.

I think it would be fair to say that most of the young men and women who hung around the square in 1972 were from middle to lower income families. With the exceptions of the Simpson brothers, all the men either currently attended or had previously attended Harrisonville High School. A few of the older men in the group had recently returned to town after completing military service and were collecting unemployment after having moved back in with their parents. A few of these returning Veterans may have been working, most were not. John Risner said when he and Gary Hale returned from duty, "we immediately started drawing unemployment…. And really having fun. . .. We hated everything back then, we hated the way everything was run, but we're just now learning to do something about it." (Eszterhas, Charlie, 20)

None of the men listed in this chapter were willing to speak with me for this book. I have listed the ages of these men at the time of the event in 1972. I have noted the high school that each attended, but for most, I am not sure if they graduated or not. Keep in mind that this time, it was not uncommon for men of this age to drop out of high school, with a plan of entering the military or to begin their working lives. I am also not listing them as a military Veteran unless I have documentation that they did indeed serve. The information listed in this chapter is as of 1972. To protect the privacy of those involved, I have not provided any information as to their current whereabouts, or their life situations that have occurred after the events of 1972.

Edwin (Win) Allen		• Age 24 • SR at Harrisonville High School in 1966
Gary Hale		• Age 24 • SR at Harrisonville High School in 1966
Steve Hale		• Age 17 • Cannot locate any yearbook images of Steve Hale in HHS Annuals
John Risner		• Age 24 • SR at Harrisonville High School in 1966 • Military Veteran
Harry Miller		• Age 21 • SR at Harrisonville High School in 1969
George Russell		• Age 24 • SR at Harrisonville High School in 1966

Figure 29: Harrisonville Hippies mentioned in public records

Elwyn "Bub" Simpson	 	• Age 23 • Charlie's younger brother • SR at Sherwood High School in 1968
Douglas Snead		• Age 17 • SR at Harrisonville High School in 1972
Jim Thompson		• Age 26 • SR at Harrisonville High School in 1964?
John Thompson		• Age 22 • SR at Harrisonville High School in 1967
Romie Thompson		• Age 18 • SR at Harrisonville High School in 1972 • Many writers of the time misspelled "Romie" as "Ronnie"

Figure 30: Harrisonville Hippies mentioned in public records

Spring 1972

It was a mild late winter and early spring in western Missouri in 1972. Temperatures were regularly in the 40s in January, the 60s in February, and the 70s in March. These warmer than usual temperatures allowed the residents of Harrisonville to get outside earlier than most years. To the local hippie group, being outside meant hanging out on the square. But the residents who enjoyed hanging out on the square were not limited to young people. There was also a regular group of retired men, likely farmers, who also enjoyed sitting on the benches at

Figure 31: Not from 1972, but still a good picture of what the square would have looked like. The biggest difference between 1972 and the current image above is that the parking lot on the back right corner of the photo was where the hotel was located. The hippies spent most of their time on the west side of the square, which is to the left of the doors seen in this photo.

the courthouse when the weather allowed. This group often was made up of two to six men who just enjoyed sitting on the benches on the south side of the courthouse, talking and enjoying the weather. It was the conflict between these two groups that ultimately led to the "hippie" problems in Harrisonville in the spring of 1972.

There was not a single significant event that started the problems between the two groups. A hippie insider described the conflict as a "slow burn". A snide comment here, a misinterpreted glance there, etc. These small things eventually evolved into a kind of open verbal warfare between the two groups. The old men would make comments such as, "get a haircut", "get a job", or "get off the square". In a later *Kansas City Star* report, some of the older hippies complained that the reason that several of them had moved back home with their parents was because "nobody would rent to us". One hippie complained, "a while back some of us rented a house, but it was under 24-hour surveillance and soon we got kicked out." (Butler, Gun Spree, 1)

In response to comments and looks from the old men, the hippies would reply with such retorts as, "make me motherfucker", "kiss my ass", or "I fought for this country, I have as much right to be here as you." Remember that the hippies were young men, several who had served in the military and came home to a town and a country that did not welcome them with fanfare and parades. They were young people trying to figure out their place in society and the town they grew up in seemed to have turned its back on them. In fact, their hometown was treating them as second-class citizens telling them how to look, dress, and where they could congregate. This real or perceived discrimination led many of the hippies to more extreme belligerent behavior. The young men would regularly challenge remarks, innocent or not, with verbal confrontations or physical posturing, such as, "Come over here and make me leave, motherfucker!".

It was quite common for the hippies to use "colorful" language in their responses to the old men. It wasn't long until the battle with the old men on the benches became a battle with all adults that frequented the square. Most interactions between the hippies and townspeople involved vulgar language on the part of the hippies. In today's world, we have been desensitized to vulgar language, but in 1972 the use of such language was not accepted by polite society.

When asked about other activities that were occurring on the square, the hippie insider told me that things like stopping traffic by playing Frisbee, yelling obscenities at older square visitors, urinating on courthouse grounds, and even having sex behind the bushes on the west side of the courthouse probably all happened. In a later police, report the investigating officer asks Bub Simpson if the hippies were having sex in the bushes. The report says that Bub, "did not deny it and would not admit having seen this or participated, however, he hesitated a long time before answering." In the same interview, Ike Simpson believed that it had happened and at one point told his boys, "If the Good Lord had wanted people to be dogs, he would have made them dogs." (Police Report)

Making vulgar comments to square visitors was another regular complaint from residents about the hippies on the square. The hippies would sit on the grass or the wall of the square and ogle and yell sexually explicit comments at all women and girls that visited the various businesses around the square. Grabbing their crotch and yelling, "Hey mama, you want some of this" was a common occurrence in the spring of 1972. It is likely this type of behavior, as much as any of the other transgressions, that led to business slowing down for square merchants. It is said that many wives and mothers no longer felt comfortable going to the square, so they simply avoided going, which was not good for square businesses. A few of the women that I interviewed related to me that their parents prohibited them from going to the square alone due to the activities of the hippie group. One anonymous interviewee, who was a regular on the square, told me that vulgar comments and images were frequently written or drawn into the dust on their vehicles. The Harrisonville Square, the hub of local commerce, was becoming a scary place.

Another problem that the hippies were creating occurred when they congregated in front of stores on the sidewalk making it difficult for patrons to enter those establishments. This practice angered the square merchants who felt they were losing business due to the large groups gathered in front of their establishments.

Eyewitnesses report that none of the prior mentioned activities happened every day but probably did occur at one point or another. When something happened once, the town rumor mill started up, and eventually residents believed that the offensive action was happening every day. The hippies were also said to purposely leave "evidence" of their debauchery on the courthouse lawn. Alcohol containers, prophylactics, and women's panties smeared with ketchup were all left directly under the window of Everett Wade, the town juvenile officer. The hippies believed that the town maintenance workers were tasked with taking all the evidence to Wade for cataloging. (Eszterhas, Charlie, 93) The general belief of both rumors and truths led the town to the conclusion, by the end of February of 1972, that Harrisonville had a hippie problem and local authorities needed to get it under control.

The older men in the hippie group were considered leaders of the group. Charlie Simpson, 25, John Risner, 24, George Russell, 24, Jim Thompson, 27, and his brother, John Thompson, 22, were all looked up to by the younger men in the group. The hippie group congregating on the square generally consisted of anywhere from 4 – 35 hippies on any given day. The group was predominantly male, but several females would also be found hanging out with them. The females were often a rotating cast of girlfriends of the men in the group. Eszterhas contends that some of the girls were passed around sexually among the older men in the group. Finding sexual partners for men in the group did not seem to be a problem as many females seemed willing to participate in this act with them. This group was considered the "cool" kids for those young people in town who considered themselves "outcasts". These kids were not football stars and cheerleaders, but they were tough and outspoken about the issues of the day. The group's "cool" vibe attracted many of the younger set who wanted to be a part of the popular counterculture movement, which they felt the hippies on the square represented.

Except for Edwin Allen, the group was comprised of all Caucasians. The fact that Edwin was the only non-white in the group should not be a surprise since African Americans as a group made up less than 1% of the city's population. African American citizens were still forced to sit in the balcony at the Lee Theater and there remained places in town where their mere presence was not allowed. The inclusion of Edwin Allen in the group lends some credibility to the group's stance on modern issues including racism, sexism, and other topics of the day. Edwin (Win) Allen, who Eszterhas called "the Ni##er" was 24 years old and had been dishonorably discharged from the United States Army for going AWOL. He was described as "birdlike" due to being very skinny, and almost frail. (Eszterhas, *Rolling Stone*, 46) People I have interviewed described him as always being strung out on drugs. This "impression" is secondhand information and none of those people knew for sure if that was true. It is said that he would loudly yell "Here come the pigs" each time he saw a law enforcement officer coming their way. (Eszterhas, *Rolling Stone*, 46) Win certainly had his eccentricities, such as the way he dressed, how he purposely slurred his words, and the large afro wig that he wore. That said, many of the people I have spoken to imply that he was a fun person to be around and like the rest of the hippies liked to push the envelope in terms of his actions toward the town and local authorities.

Racism existed in Harrisonville, Missouri in 1972. Similar racist beliefs were duplicated in thousands of small towns all over the country, it was not just a Harrisonville issue. Racism pervaded a significant portion of the country. The fact that Win Allen was African American and was one of the key perpetrators of the problem on the square fed into those racist beliefs and made matters worse. There are unverified stories about Win having sex with underage, white girls, in a van parked at the courthouse. No one can confirm that sexual intercourse happened, but many witnesses confirm he would regularly be seen holding hands and necking with girls on the courthouse grass. There is another story of Win and an unnamed white girl getting in a van and rocking the van up and down just to give the impression that they were having sex. Win was again finding a way to antagonize Harrisonville residents by making them believe that sex was happening in that van, even though it was not.   In her 1982 article in *The Kansas State Collegian*, Harrisonville resident Eva Wilson, who was 15 at the time, remembers that her family and friends viewed the square as a "wicked place at the time" and avoided going there if at all possible. (Wilson, 1)

Edwin played the race card frequently; at times it was likely justified. Volumes have been written about race relations in the United States and this book will not delve deeply into that topic. Suffice to say, racial equity was certainly a societal problem in 1972. Win, like most African Americans, suffered due to his race but he also seemed to derive a certain amount of pleasure using his race to anger residents of Harrisonville. If his goal was to do things that would get under the skin of the white citizens and the local authorities of Harrisonville? Mission accomplished.

At their meeting on March 15th, in response to this "hippie problem", the Harrisonville City Council passed a new set of ordinances to give the local police more authority to deal with the situation on the square. The large bushes around the courthouse were cut down and several new ordinances were passed that appeared to be aimed directly at the hippies.

The new ordinances included the following:
- The use of vulgar language, profane or indecent language was declared illegal.

- It was now illegal for a group of persons to assemble or collect on any sidewalk obstructing the free passage of others.
- It was now illegal to deface or destroy any public or private property or tamper with any fire hydrant or fire alarm.
- Restrictions against "Peeping Toms"
- Restrictions against picketing or parades

The penalties for violating these new ordinances included a fine of not more than $500 or imprisonment in the county jail for not more than 60 days, or some combination of the two. (Law Enforcement, 1)

In later quotes and articles written about the enacting and enforcing of these new rules, some have cited an ordinance that prohibited loitering in groups of three or more. *The Wildcat News* published an emotional editorial comparing this ordinance to Jim Crow laws stating,

If this new ordinance is to be enforced in this manner— prohibiting young people from loitering, not elderly ones, then this ordinance will be much like black-segregation laws of the past. (Proposed City Ordinance)

The problem with their stance is that there was no "three-person loitering" rule passed as part of the package of new ordinances. To the paper's credit, in their edition the next month, the students at *The Wildcat News* published a "clarification" in their paper which clarified that the only loitering rule passed recently was passed by the City Council 5 years earlier in 1967. The 1967 ordinance allowed police to disburse groups of loiterers inside the city limits. (New City Ordinance) Even in the 1967 rule, there is no mention of a 3-person rule. That is not to say that the Harrisonville police did not use the 1967 ordinance as justification to disburse groups of young people, including the hippies, but, at least officially, no "3-person" ordinance ever existed. Defending the actions taken by the City Council, Alderman Hacker said,

If there has been a question of harassment of these youths, they provoked it. We're not taking sides. We're drafting laws to keep law and order. There is only one question: do they act as they please, or do they act in conjunction with other people? (Wilks, 8)

One of the "final straws", according to local filling station owner, John Leach, was an afternoon on the square where the Hippie group decided to play Frisbee in the street and block traffic for over two hours. According to Leach, a couple of the Frisbee players, who were the sons and daughters of the local "establishment", were arrested by the Harrisonville Police. Leach contended that the parents of these young people immediately rushed up to the police station and chastised Chief Davis and his staff for "harassing" them. Leach opined that this event "marked the decline of the police force, the hands of law enforcement were tied by the city fathers." (Floyd) No charges were filed, which further frustrated the citizenry.

Skirmish at Sears

Thursday, April 20, 1972, is when the spark that eventually led to bloodshed occurred. The hippies and several high schoolers, "teeny bros", were up on the square making posters and talking up a storm about their plans for an anti-war parade on the square. During the upcoming weekend, G.M. Allen was hosting a meeting of the Firefighters Association of Missouri in Harrisonville. A parade was planned for 2 pm, Saturday in which over 40 area Missouri fire departments would be showing off their trucks by parading them around the square. Large crowds were expected to come and see the fire truck parade and then spend their money in the shops. The hippies planned to hijack Allen's parade by marching, chanting, and passing out leaflets about the atrocities of the Vietnam War.

That Thursday afternoon was a pleasant, sunny, 75-degree day in Harrisonville. After a day of making plans and creating posters, etc., the elder hippie crowd, Win Allen, 24, Harry Miller, 21, George Russell, 24, John Thompson, 22, Gary Hale, 24, had decided that they needed something to drink and picked some of the younger crowd to go over to South Side Drug Store and get them a carton of soda. Several of the "younger hippies" were tasked with getting the drinks. The "teeny bros" likely included Steve Hale, 17, Romie Thompson, 18, and Doug Snead, 17, all of whom were arrested and included in the court documents filed after the event.

Beginning from their roost on the west side of the courthouse, the group of young and older hippies meandered across the street taking up a post near a mailbox that stood on the corner in front of the Sears Store and South Side Drug Store. The younger kids were sent inside to get the drinks while the others waited outside on the sidewalk. While waiting for their drinks, Don Foster, manager of the Sears store, pulled up in his car directly in front of the Sears store and demanded that the group move away from the front of his store as they were blocking entry to the store for his customers. Don's father, Lloyd Foster, owned South Side Drug which was located right next door to his son's Sears Store.

Figure 32: Sears Store and south side of square in 1972. South Side Drug Store is to the immediate east of the Sears store.   (Photo Courtesy of David Atkinson)

Harry Miller told Joe Eszterhas the story this way:

…out of nowhere, Don Foster drives up. Man, I seen that car coming, you could tell he was gonna do something, it was in his eyes, like he already knew he was gonna do this. . . So he storms up and he starts saying – 'Get away from my store!' He says to Win – 'Get your black ass out of here!' So he starts violently throwing shit and John Thompson says – 'Listen man, we pay taxes, I'm not getting out of here.' So the Foster dude says – 'Oh, you wanna fight? I'll fight you!' So he pushes John with both hands, just pushes John and knocks him back. John weighs about forty pounds less than the dude and most his weight is stuck up on top of his head in his hair. Well, right then I caught a sense . . . I knew exactly what was going to happen. Okay, so then the old man, Lloyd, comes running out and starts throwing some bogus shit. I don't know what he was saying, just yelling and screaming. Somehow Don Foster got ahold of John again and pushed him again.

So I got between them. I says to Foster –'Man, leave us alone, you're trying to fight us, you wanna get us throwed in jail, just leave our asses alone, we're not going to jail for you.' And he says – 'You get out of the way or I'll smack your ass, buddy!' So I got out of the way and they got off by theirselves[sic] again and started piling at it. So his father, old Lloyd, says – 'By Gawd, I'm gonna call the police!' So he walks back to his store, takes about four steps, doesn't even get to his phone, turns back out again watching them hassle, and here comes the police already turning the corner of the courthouse, boogeying from the courthouse. (Eszterhas, Charlie, 36)

By the time the Harrisonville Police officers, Jim Harris, Francis Wirt, and Donald Marler arrived, John Thompson and Don Foster were down on the ground and according to Miller,

[Don] Foster is "smacking" (punching?) Thompson in the head. Thompson is trying to defend himself by grabbing at Foster's neck and head. Sergeant Jim Harris immediately engages and, according to Miller, bends down at an odd angle so that he can hit Thompson with his billy club.   He delivers blows to Thompson's face and shoulder at which time Foster rolls off and allows the police officers to grab Thompson and lift him upright.

Old Lloyd starts pointing at us saying 'Him! And Him! And Him! And then points to Win and says – 'The Ni##er! The Ni##er! The Ni##er! Over and over again. So the pigs put us all under arrest and started walking us over to the jail in the Sheriff's office. (Eszterhas, *Rolling Stone*, 47)

On the way to the jail, Miller says that one of the "pigs" poked Win Allen in the side with his nightstick. Allen turned to glare at the "pig", according to Miller yelled, "The Ni##er is resisting arrest!"   This additional charge of resisting arrest would be added to the initial charge of disturbing the peace for Win Allen. Was Allen targeted because he was black or just because he was Win "here come the pigs" Allen?   I think it is fair to say that Win was not a popular person with local authorities. The other seven hippies would be charged with only disturbing the peace.

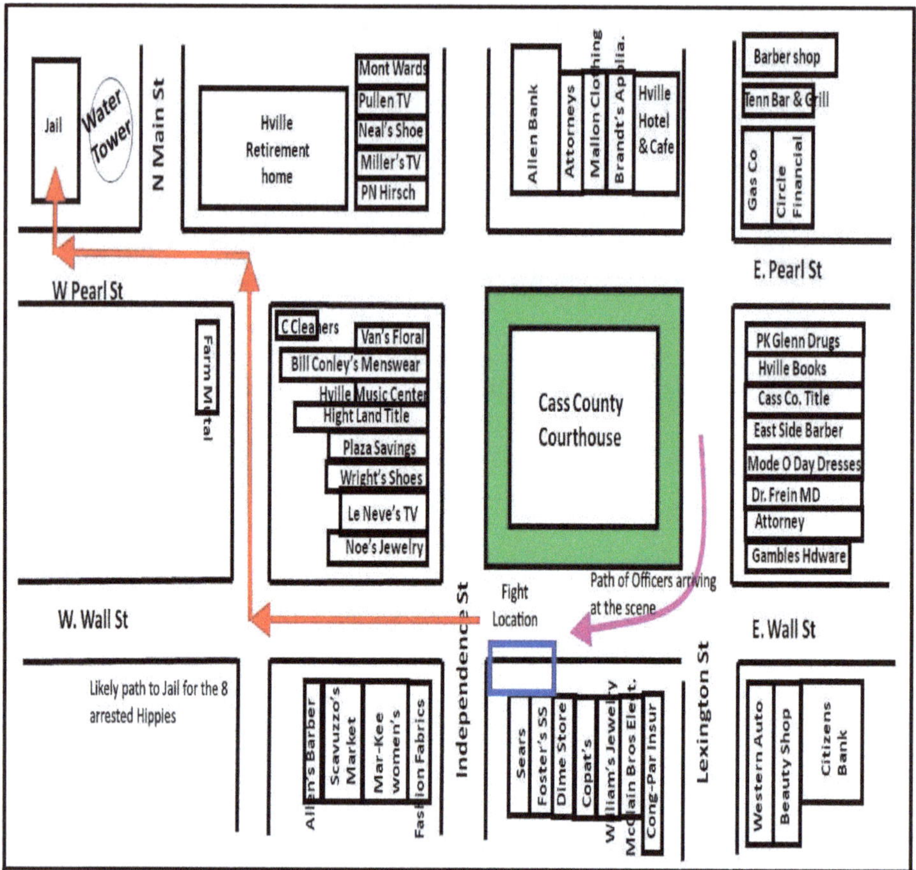

Figure 33: Details of the altercation in front of the Sears Store between the hippies and Don and Lloyd Foster on Thursday, April 23, 1972. Pink lines show the path of the officers arriving at the scene and the red lines show the path of the arrestees being marched to the jail.

When the arrestees and the officers arrived at the jail on West Pearl Street, the hippies were thrown into a cell. According to Miller's account, the jail was not the most luxurious of accommodations. Bail was set for each arrestee at $110 for disturbing the peace. Win Allen's bail was set to $1,110 due to $1,000 being added for resisting arrest.

Immediately upon their arrival in the jail cell, the group of hippies started yelling that they wanted to file a complaint against Don Foster for assaulting John Thompson. Initially, Miller says that both Chief Davis and Sergeant Harris said that they did not have the authority to take a complaint. The hippies kept yelling and eventually the officers brought the city attorney to the jail to "take their complaint". The hippie's version is that the city attorney gave them two sheets of paper with the words "Municipal Court" at the top and some other "bogus printed stuff" on them. The hippies were asked to sign their names, but nothing regarding their actual complaint was written on the paper. (Eszterhas, Charlie, 38)

Arrestee/Age	Charge	Bail
Win Allen/24	Disturbing the Peace Resisting Arrest	$1,110
Gary Hale/24	Disturbing the Peace	$110
Harry Miller/21	Disturbing the Peace	$110
George Russell/24	Disturbing the Peace	$110
John Thompson/22	Disturbing the Peace	$110
Steve Hale/17	Disturbing the Peace	$110
Doug Snead/17	Disturbing the Peace	$110
Romie Thompson/17	Disturbing the Peace	$110

Figure 34: Source Kansas City Times, June 6, 1972

   The incident was noteworthy among area law enforcement officials in the area. In his recounting of the tale, Miller says that at certain points in the evening, they saw six different Missouri State Highway patrolmen, five local Harrisonville officers, five officers from the sheriff's department and even the Cass County Game Warden checked in to see if any help was needed. (Eszterhas, Charlie, 39)

   In his book, Eszterhas recounts a few more stories about the evening. The stories were reportedly told to the author by Harry Miller. The first is about a 16-year-old dropout who was the current girlfriend of one of the hippies in the jail. The young lady had witnessed the arrest and followed the group to the jail where the city fire truck was parked outside with firemen reportedly on the truck holding axes. The young lady stood in front of the truck and was repeatedly screaming, "You fuckin Pigs!". When the teen saw her mother pull up, she took off running down the alley between the sheriff's office and the retirement home. At this time the firefighters trained their firehose on the young girl and unleashed a powerful burst of water that sent her skidding to the gravel roadway on her face. This story seems far-fetched, and I initially doubted it's accuracy. I doubted it until several other persons that I interviewed confirmed that this incident did take place.

The second story concerns G.M. Allen who was considered one of the primary adversaries of the hippies. G.M. was the fire chief and it was his men that reportedly were in the truck in the previous incident. Miller reportedly told Eszterhas that G.M. Allen entered the jail and asked "Where's the Ni##er? I got something to say to the Ni##er." Upon seeing Win Allen, Chief Allen said, "Win, I want you to come see me tomorrow about that bill you owe me." Win contends that the "bill" that G.M. Allen was referring to was a loan that his family had with the Citizens Bank where G.M. Allen served as president. The assumption here is that G.M. Allen was threatening to "call in the loan" that Win's family had with his bank, thus making his family pay for Win's deeds. (Eszterhas, Charlie, 40)

I can find no evidence of this happening. That does not mean it didn't happen, but I have found no evidence to corroborate this story. To be fair, the chances of finding actual evidence of this event are highly unlikely. This situation is common in Eszterhas' retelling of the events. He includes a great deal of secondhand information with no sources to back the stories up. This is not a criticism of Eszterhas, as his main sources were conversations with the participants and thus there would be no documentation to confirm a given story. I think it is very likely that Harry Miller did relate this story to the writer, but with no way to corroborate them, the reader will have to decide if they choose to believe the story, as told, or not.

The hippies spent the night in the jail with one of them making calls to parents and friends to try to get someone to come up and bail them out. According to *The Cass County Democrat-Missourian*, Steve Hale was bailed out that same night and the Thompson brothers, John and Romie, were bailed out early the next morning. That left five hippies still in custody. This means that five sets of parents had made the decisions not to bail their wayward offspring out of jail. At 11:00 am the next day, Friday, April 21, Charlie Simpson sauntered into the Harrisonville Jail, plopped down $1,550 in cash, and proclaimed, "Simpson's the name, revolution's my game. Free the People!"

One interesting point about this event pertains to the story Eszterhas tells and the story in the papers regarding John Risner. In his book, Joe Eszterhas says that Risner was one of the eight men arrested. He even goes as far as to tell a story about an altercation between Charlie and another man as Risner is being released from his cell. The problem is that John Risner was not one of the men arrested. The arrest and subsequent trial were reported in multiple court documents and none of those documents mention John Risner as having been one of the men arrested. It is possible that Risner was with Charlie Simpson when he went to the Sheriff's office to bail out his friends, but I find no evidence that Risner was incarcerated with the other men during this incident as the book claims. It is possible that Eszterhas may have confused "John" Risner, with "John" Thompson, who was arrested in the incident.

Blood in the Streets

Readers should be aware that there are some inconsistencies in existing accounts regarding this event. In my early research, the facts surrounding events such as where Simpson got out of the car, who was driving, etc., were clear. Most of the documents that I uncovered agreed with the facts for these parts of the story. It was clear, that is, until I received the official Missouri State Police report through a Public Information Request. The State Police report threw me for a bit of a loop in that it did not align with what I had read in most of the information available including newspaper reports and Eszterhas' writing.

The story told by the media at the time was quite different from the one told in the police report, not in terms of the major events but more regarding the peripheral details of how it all went down. Looking at the various sources, it is my opinion that the media at the time was taking rumors and secondhand accounts and reporting them as fact. Over time, those rumors became fact because nobody came forward to dispute them. After reading the police report, I think it tells the true story. The report is very detailed and thorough and seems to have interviews with all the people who would know the details. It does call into question which parts of the media reports and the events reported by Eszterhas can be believed as truth. I will try and point out significant differences between sources where they exist.

Once all the arrestees were bailed out of jail, Charlie and the hippies gathered at George Russell's house to make plans for their demonstration the next day on the square. It was important that the rally still be held the next day so they could take advantage of the crowds created by the fire truck parade. Now they would not only be protesting the war but also the unfair policies of the Harrisonville authorities. Jim Thompson remembers Charlie being in a good mood laughing and calling the others "jailbirds" as they were preparing for the protest.

Charlie left George Russell's house early in the afternoon to go back to Holden and arrange to have the flyers, that the group had created, printed so they could pass them out at the protest the next day.   At around 3 pm that afternoon, Simpson and Risner, found themselves sitting alongside Highway 58 with car trouble. Luckily for them, a former hippie friend, Russell Honley, 23, stopped and picked them up. Honley, a Harrisonville resident, and college student, was on his way home from classes at Central Missouri State University in Warrensburg. Risner and Simpson asked Honley to take them to Harrisonville.

Upon their arrival in Harrisonville, Honley ran a few errands and then Simpson asked him to take them back to Holden so Simpson could pick up some things he needed for the evening. According to the State Police report Honley agreed to this and they started back to Holden. It's important to note that Honley's name is only mentioned in the police report. It is not present in any other documentation that I have found.

Back in Holden, Simpson grabbed his sleeping bag, his M-1 rifle, and a large amount of ammunition. He told Risner and Honley that he planned to do some target practice at North Lake. When the trio arrived back in town, they immediately went out to North Lake where Simpson stashed the sleeping bag in some brush telling his friend that he planned on sleeping there that night after the target practice session. The three men then got in the car and headed back to town to find a group of friends who were going to join them in the shooting practice. Honley was still driving, Simpson was in the passenger seat and Risner was in the back seat. The M-1 rifle was on the floorboard of the car at Simpson's feet and the ammunition was in his jacket pockets.

After driving around town a few times looking for their friends, they ended up on the square where, after circling a couple of times, they left the square heading north on Lexington Street, just east of the Harrisonville Hotel. Honley then turned left (west) into the alley directly behind the hotel. About halfway through the block, Simpson grabbed the gun off the floorboard and jumped out of the slow-moving car. Wearing a drab green army jacket, muddy boots, and ratty jeans, Simpson ran west cutting across the Allen Bank drive-through lane. This would be the last time Honley and Risner would see their friend alive.

Most media accounts say that Risner was driving his car, a red Volkswagen Beetle, with Simpson in the passenger seat. Those accounts have Simpson leaving the vehicle just north of the square near the exit of the Allen Bank drive through. The differences between the media accounts and the police report are hard to reconcile. Russell is not even mentioned in any media accounts, but in the police report, he

Figure 35: View of the drive-through of the Allen Bank building. According to the police report, Simpson jumped out of the car about where this image was taken from and ran through the drive-through lanes across Independence Street. (Photo taken by author December 2022)

is a central figure in the overall story. I can't explain the differences. In this case, we can't just blame Eszterhas for tweaking the story for his needs because all other media sources also ignore any involvement by Russell Honley.

As if this discrepancy is not confusing enough, I later interviewed Ray White who was standing right next to Charlie Simpson when the shots were fired. Ray remembers the car, a Volkswagen Beetle, was driving "south" on Independence Street and Simpson got out about 100 feet north of the intersection of Pearl Street and Independence Street. Ray did not see this but rather heard it as he was facing the other direction. White's recollection more closely follows the media reports except for which way the car was going.

On this point, I'm going to tell the story as per the police report. I'm making this choice only because it is the official record. I suppose it is possible that witnesses, primarily Risner and Honley, changed the story they told to the police to distance themselves from Simpson and what he did. In the grand scheme of things, the facts about where Simpson got out of the car and who was driving have very little impact on the overall story. As a researcher, I'm frustrated that I can't pin down exactly what happened but wanted to ensure that the reader is aware that there are multiple versions of this aspect of the story.

After leaving the car midway through the alley, Simpson cut across the Allen Bank drive- through-lane, jammed a 30-round clip into his weapon, and quickly cut across Independence to the corner in front of the PN Hirsch Store. At the same time, local businessmen Ray White and Don Ament, and Cass County Prosecuting Attorney, Charles Hight, had just met on the corner of the sidewalk in front of the Allen Bank. The three friends were standing in a semi-circle facing east waiting for Officers Wirt and Marler to arrive so that they could question them on what happened at the Sears store the night before. The three men were friends with Officer Marler. They were acquainted with Officer Wirt, but he had only been on the job for a month, and they did not know him quite as well.

When the officers arrived, they joined the semi-circle with their backs to the glass windows of the bank after which Ray White felt someone nudge past him. Simpson was already raising his gun when he entered the small group of friends. He raised his gun and turned it on the officers who were standing with their backs to the glass windows of the

Figure 36: Allen Bank on the northwest corner of the square in 1972. The P.N. Hirsch Store in the image is across N. Independence St. It is on the corner, almost directly below the Allen Bank sign, where Officers Marler and Wirt were gunned down. (Photo courtesy of David Atkinson)

bank. He first fired several shots at Officer Wirt, who fell to the sidewalk.

Simpson then turned the gun on Officer Marler and fired several point-blank shots into his body. Officer Marler staggered back and leaned against the corner post of the bank building with his hands covering wounds in his abdomen. The shooter then swung the gun back to Wirt and fired a few more shots into the dying officer. As Simpson brought the weapon back to Marler, the officer was heard pleading, "Oh God no, please no". (White). Officer Marler's pleas went unanswered as Simpson fired several shots at the already wounded man. Both officers had wounds to their hands which were likely inflicted as they held their hands up to protect themselves from the second round of shots. After the last round of shots, Officer Marler staggered away from the building and fell into the street right next to the curb with his head facing north. Ray White, who was standing just a few feet from the shooter recalls, "They (Marler and Wirt) had their back to the glass of the bank, and he just stood there shooting back and forth between them. Francis fell at my feet." (Minich, 1) Both officers died with their weapons still snapped into their holsters.

It is possible, following the police's version of events, that Simpson had seen Officers Marler and Wirt heading west on the north side of the square when the car with the three hippies inside had left the square going north on Lexington Street just a few minutes earlier.   The fact that Simpson ignored the group of businessmen on the corner makes it clear that Simpson was targeting the officers.

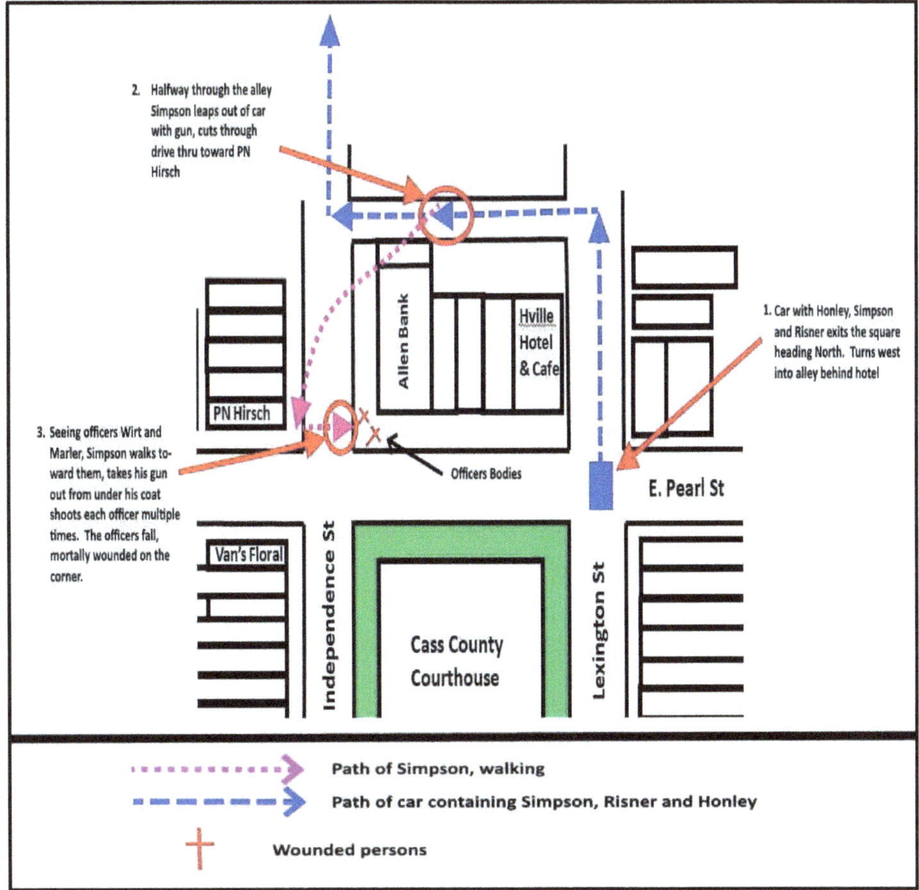

After Simpson left the car in the alley, Risner and Honley told police that they heard shots, got scared, and turned the car north on Independence Street heading away from the square. The shots that the two men had heard were their friend, Charlie, gunning down the two officers in front of the Allen Bank.

Immediately after firing the second round of shots into the officers, Simpson turned and entered the Allen Bank. Once inside the lobby of the bank, he began spraying bullets into the back wall of the bank. When Simpson entered the bank, Charles Hight and Don Ament immediately ran across Independence Street and entered Hight's father's title business. Ray White was frozen and didn't flee with his friend immediately. Instead, he remembers looking into the bank through the glass and seeing Simpson spraying bullets into the back wall.

At one point White remembers locking eyes with Simpson as he

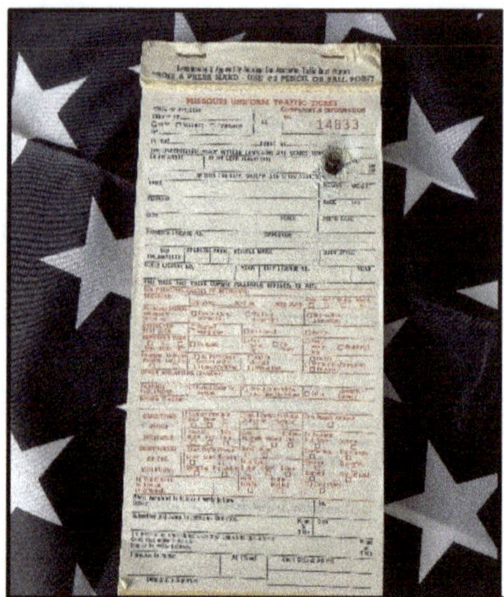

Figure 37:   Officer Donald Marler's ticket book with bullet hole. (Image courtesy of the Marler Family)

turned and looked out the window, saying, "I will never forget him looking out the window at me. He was shooting and looking right at me. He could have shot me through the glass." (Minich, 1) It is at this point that White heard his friends yelling at him to take cover.

Inside the bank, two young ladies, Mary Ellen Stuart and a pregnant woman, Mrs. Deborah Roach, were finishing up their day at the bank. When Simpson started firing, they both took cover behind their desks. Mary Ellen Stuart told *The Kansas City Times*,

I didn't recognize the sound, I thought it was a car backfiring or something. Then I looked up into the lobby and saw him standing in front, firing back at us. I pushed Mrs. Roach down behind my desk. When the shooting stopped Mrs. Roach said, I think I've been shot. (She had blood on the side of her dress) After the man left, I stood up and saw that I had blood on my side and realized I'd been shot, too. (Death Swift, 1)

Simpson did not appear to be aiming his shots at anyone, rather he was just spraying them randomly into the back wall. Allen Bank Senior Vice President, Doyle P. Lindsey told police that Simpson was in the bank for no more than five or six seconds and didn't say a word while in the bank. The official report says that police found 9 shell casings inside the bank lobby.

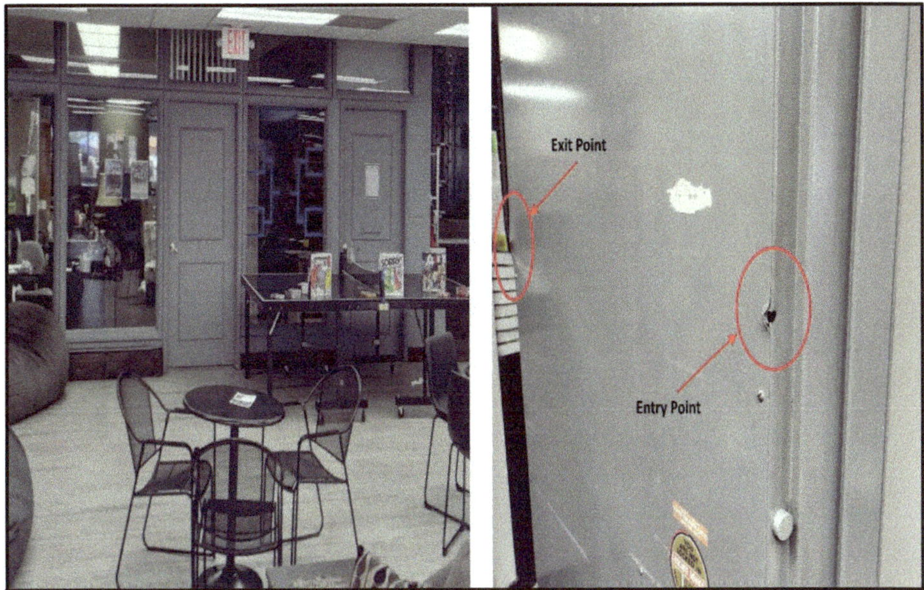

Figure 38:(Left) This image shows the present-day interior of the Allen Bank Building, which is now a Youth Center. Left: A view of the back wall of the bank. (Right) The open vault, which was behind the door on the left in the first image, was hit by a bullet that went straight through the vault door. The bullet holes and vault are still present today.

Why Allen Bank? I must admit that as a young man and when I first started researching this event, I had always thought that Simpson went into the "Allen Bank" to get back at G.M. Allen for all the trouble Allen had made for the hippies on the square. The problem with that theory is that G.M. Allen did not own the Allen Bank. Instead, he was an officer of the Citizens Bank just off the opposite corner of the square. Did Charlie know that? Or like me, did he think G.M. owned the Allen Bank? My guess is that Simpson knew that G.M. Allen did not work at Allen Bank. As much interaction as the hippies had with Mr. Allen, I surmise that they would have seen Mr. Allen coming and going from the Citizens Bank daily and thus would have known at which bank Mr. Allen worked. For that reason, I think the theory that Charlie was mistaken about who owned Allen Bank is incorrect.

Figure 39: Left: This image shows the inside of the teller station. Red circles show bullet holes Right: This image shows the outside of the teller station inside the bank. The red circles show the bullet holes. (Photo Courtesy of Missouri State Police)

Instead, my theory, which is only that, a theory, is that Charlie decided to shoot the officers when the three hippies passed them walking their beat as they left the square in Honley's car. When Charlie leaped out of the car in the alley, his intent was to shoot the officers. Once he had accomplished that goal, the closest door was that of the Allen Bank and he went in and sprayed bullets inside that business. If he had not met the officers on that specific corner, he may well have entered the door of another business and sprayed shots into that business. We will never know for sure. I believe that once Charlie fired his first shots at the two officers, any semblance of a plan went out the window. Mayor Raine was probably correct when he later told reports that Simpson simply went "berserk".

Leaving the bank, Simpson went out the door past the fallen officers and took several wild shots at a zigzagging Ray White, who after coming to his senses, began running in a zig zag pattern diagonally across the street. White was not hit, but bullet holes in cars parked in that area prove that Simpson had taken at least a few shots at him as he ran southwest across Independence Street. This short burst of shots helps to clarify a problem that I had with the story as told by people on the square at the time. Several people told me that there was an initial burst of shots, then a long delay then another burst. This didn't jive with the story as I knew it. Most accounts do not mention a second burst of shots. The second burst that people heard was likely the shots taken at Ray White as he ran across the street.

After shooting at White, Simpson headed down Pearl Street to the west, toward the sheriff's office. Did he go this way purposely to "hunt" Sheriff Gough at the jail, or was that just the nearest exit off the square? I'm not sure you can apply rhyme or reason to his actions at this point. It certainly is possible that he was targeting the sheriff and/or his deputies, just as he may have targeted Officers Marler and Wirt. Keep in mind that he had just interacted with the sheriff and his staff that very morning when he bailed his friends out of jail.

After crossing Independence Street, Simpson continued down West Pearl Street, which slopes gently to the west and led to the jail. Simpson descended the slope passing the Harrisonville Retirement Home on his right and Capitol Cleaners on his left. Seeing movement to his left, Simpson turned and opened fire on an unsuspecting Orville Allen, 58, who was getting out of his truck intending to go into the cleaners. Mr. Allen managed Allen Cleaners in Garden City and Dorothy's Laundry in Grandview and was just stopping by the Capitol Cleaners on his regular routine to deliver some cleaning to the Harrisonville shop.

Simpson fired at least four times at Mr. Allen hitting him once in the chest and once in the leg. Two other bullets were found embedded in his truck. Mr. and Mrs. Ray Stewart, the owners of Capitol Cleaners, were horrified as they witnessed the shooting of Mr. Allen looking on from inside their cleaning business. Unknown until later is that Allen's two daughters, Linda, and Sharon, both in their 20s, were on the square at the time their father was gunned down. The daughters who were picking up some medicine, heard shots and hurried to get away from the square. They saw the bodies of the two officers as they were leaving the square and assumed that the bank had been robbed. They would find a note waiting for them when they arrived home in Garden City to hurry to the hospital in Harrisonville as their father had been shot. They wondered why the bank robber had shot their father. (Bradley, A6)

As Mr. Allen fell, mortally wounded, to the ground, Simpson continued down the street toward the jail where Sheriff Gough had just gotten off work for the day and was sitting down with his wife, Betty, for dinner. Fortunately, his 14-year-old son, Ron, was not home.   The sheriff's living quarters were in the front of the jail at the time. Hearing the strange noise, Gough stepped out the front door of his residence to see Simpson coming at him shooting.

What I heard didn't sound like gunfire.   I thought it was someone beating a piece of tin with a stick. When I stepped outside, I saw him coming around the corner of the nursing home, firing at me. (Butler, Discord, 2A)

Figure 40: 2022 Image of the building that housed the Cass County jail in 1972, while still standing, does not currently serve that purpose.   This image shows the jail in 2022.   The section with the red X was not present in 1972.   Instead, that spot was occupied by the Harrisonville water tower. The small arrow shows the door to the sheriff's residence at the time.

Sheriff Gough got several feet out of his front door before he realized what was happening. The first of Simpson's bullets struck him in the right shoulder and knocked him to the ground. He staggered to his feet and began to run back toward the safety of the jail. On his way, he took another bullet to his thigh. Finally making it back to the jail, he got inside where he forced his wife to the ground for her safety. The police reports say that eleven shots went into the jail; seven hit the open metal door and four hit the plate glass window beside that metal door.

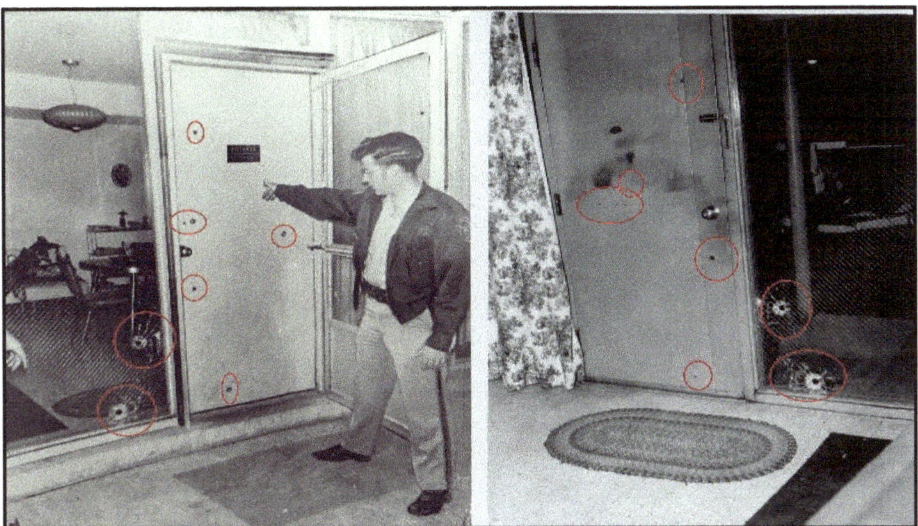

Figure 41: The image on the left shows the door to the sheriff's residence in 1972, with Sheriff's Deputy Benny Odom pointing to the bullet holes in the door; the image to the right shows the same door from the inside of the sheriff's residence.

Figure 42: The image above shows the front of the sheriff's office in 1972 (left) and today (right). After the addition of the new jail, a small entryway was constructed. The sheriff's residence door is just through the door in the image on the right and to the left. In 1972, the door to the residence would have been visible from both Pearl Street and North Main Street, which is the alley between the retirement home and the jail.

After the sheriff made it back into his residence, Simpson turned and went south into a parking area across the street south and west of the Farmers Insurance office, which was located in a small building directly across the street from the jail. A short distance into that parking area, the shooter turned and aimed his weapon back at the sheriff's office and pulled the trigger. This time the gun did not fire. Whether it was out of ammunition or was just a misfire, we do not know. Simpson then ran around the back of the Farmers Insurance building, then back to Pearl Street heading toward the Harrisonville Retirement Home. The police report quotes an eyewitness as saying that at this point it looked as if Simpson had trouble loading his gun. Other witnesses maintain that Simpson tried to enter the retirement home through a couple of the exterior doors. It is worth noting that just that morning, the retirement facility had decided to keep the exterior doors of the facility locked to protect their residents from the problems happening on the square.

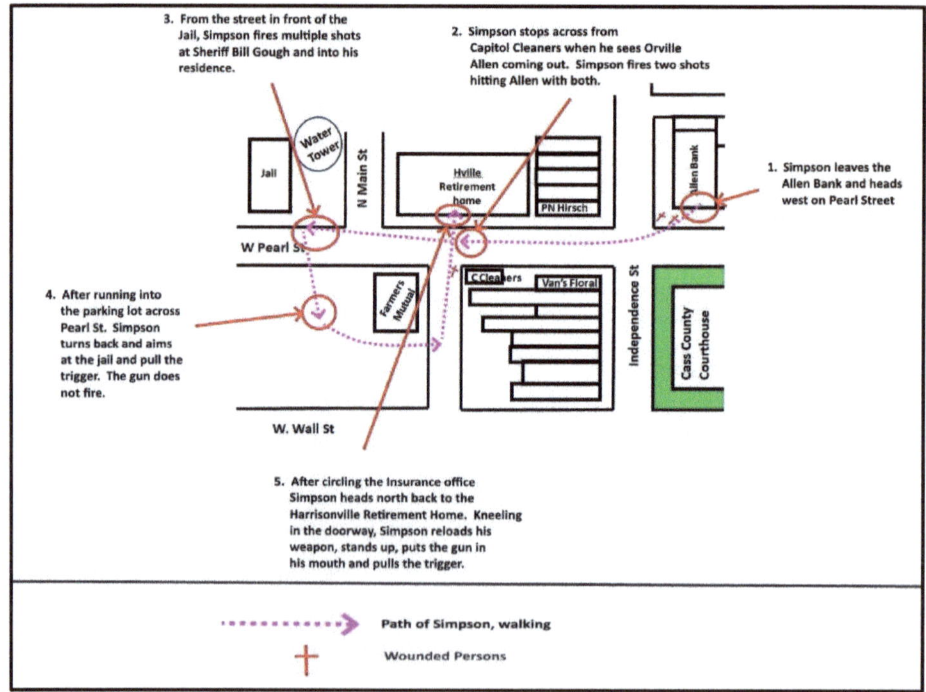

A police eyewitness says that he saw Simpson in the doorway of the retirement home, kneeling on one knee trying to get his gun reloaded. It was at this point that Ray White, on hands and knees, peeked around the corner of Van's Floral on the corner of Independence and Pearl. Sirens were just beginning to sound and White remembers Simpson raising his head and looking directly at him. White was afraid that Simpson was going to come after him. In hindsight, Mr. White thinks that Simpson probably heard the sirens and was looking up to see if he could see where the sirens were coming from. (White interview) Once Simpson had the gun loaded, he stood up, placed the barrel of the gun in his mouth, and pulled the trigger. His body fell across the sidewalk with his feet still in the doorway. "The bullet had entered the roof of the mouth and exited near the top and back of his head." (Police Report, 3)

After seeing Simpson fall, Ray White ran back across the street to Don Marler, knelt, and raised his head to his lap. Ray remembers that he knew Marler was dying; he was not a doctor, but just felt sure that Officer Marler was not going to make it. During our interview, tears came to his eyes as he remembered comforting his friend and saying, ". . . you are okay, the ambulance is on the way," he continued, "but I was lying. He died while I was holding his head in my hands." (Minich, 5A) Another eyewitness, Mike Noe, who arrived on the scene shortly after the shooting made a similar comment when he said that "I just knew by looking at them that they were dead." (Noe Interview)

Figure 43: (Left) Picture taken in the mid-1990s of the Harrisonville Retirement Home (previously a hospital). The red circle shows the location of Simpson's body after the self-inflicted gunshot. The body was laying with feet on the door sill and head facing the camera location to the southwest. (photo courtesy of Brett Jones) (Right) This photo shows the same doorway after the shooting, with Officer Benny Odom on the left, an unknown state policeman on the right, and possibly an FBI agent in the center.

From start to finish, the entire event took less than five minutes. Police estimate that Simpson fired between 35 and 40 rounds. Thirty-five shell casings were recovered at the scene. The original police drawing of the event and the property record included in the police report can be found in the Appendix.

Was this the end Simpson had planned all along? We will never know for sure.

WARNING: The images of Charlie Simpson's body after death on the following page are graphic and may be disturbing to some readers.

Page Intentionally Left Blank

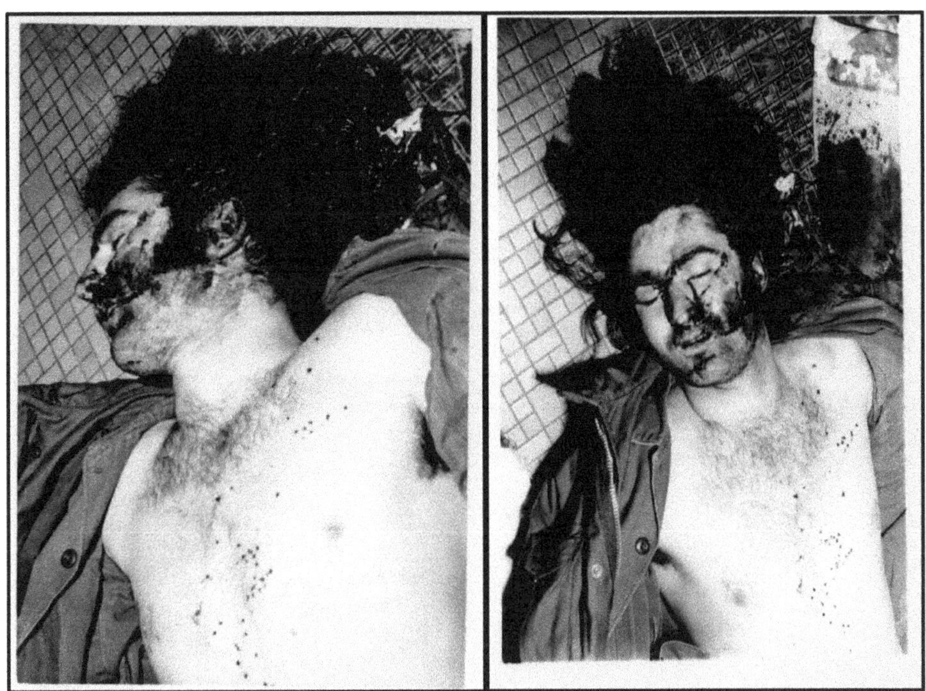

Figure 44: Harrisonville Square shooter, Charles Richard Simpson, a short time after taking his own life on West Pearl Street. (Images Courtesy of Missouri State Police)

Motive

Why did Charlie Simpson do it? Writers who have written about the incident have varied opinions as to his motive. We will never know for sure. In this section I'm going to present some of the theories that have been proposed as to why Simpson did what he did on that fateful day.

Charlie went to the bank in Holden early Friday morning and withdrew his life savings. It is said that he was saving this money to buy 13-acres of land from a farmer in Johnson County, Missouri. His friends say that Charlie's dream was to purchase this land so he and his brothers could live free from police harassment and the many problems of the world. The deal for this land, wherever it was located, had actually fallen through several days earlier when the owner rejected Simpson's offer saying that "he didn't want to sell to a hippie". On that Friday morning, Charlie used almost all his savings to bail his friends, who were arrested the night before, out of the Harrisonville Jail. In a later police interview, Bub says that Charlie didn't think he would ever get the bail money back. This seems a bit strange as Charlie was a regular participant of the criminal justice system and should have known how the bail process worked and that he would eventually get this money back. However, if he did think that using this money to bail his friends out of jail ended any possibility of owning land, this could have added to the frustration and hopelessness that Simpson had with society. This mental state of hopelessness may have pushed him closer to a mindset in which he would be willing to take multiple lives and eventually his own. Many reporters cite the "death of the dream" to own land as the reason for Charlie's actions.

Did Simpson always intend to take his own life at the end of his shooting spree? Or did the shooting spree go further than he intended, at which point he realized that what he had done would mean that he would spend the rest of his life in prison? Could this have been what he was thinking when he decided that taking his own life was his only option at that point? In direct contradiction to his actions on that Friday,

Jim Thompson is quoted as saying that just days before the shooting, Simpson had told him that, "no revolution was possible now—we'd just get shot down. We've got to work within the system." (Jones, 1)

Simpson's friends had thoughts about why he might have taken the steps that he did. Winn Allen said that he felt that Charlie was sacrificing his life so that the merchants and news media would take notice of the oppression and injustice that was happening in Harrisonville. When John Risner was asked later, "What about the people killed and their wives and kids? Don't you care about that?"

Risner replied, "Well you know, how can I criticize it. It's Charlie's thing. Like, it was a far-out thing to do." (Eszterhas, *Rolling Stone*, 52)

Janice Maloney was shocked when she heard of the events on the square, she assumed that it was Simpson's brother, Elwyn, rather than Charlie who had committed these horrendous acts. She could not imagine the Charlie Simpson she knew would do something like that. She surmised that the pressure of being an unofficial leader of this group of hippies on the square, finally got to him and he cracked. (Maloney, Interview)

Simpson's brother Elwyn believed that Charlie shot Officers Marler and Wirt, not as individuals, but rather as symbols of policy harassment and oppression. The bank was shot up because the bank represented "the greed of people".

The Kansas City Star quotes an unnamed female teenager who reportedly hung around with the hippies on the square as saying,

Charles had told several people in Harrisonville that he planned to 'shoot up the square'. He talked often about walking around the square shooting people, then taking his own life so the police could not get him." This same unnamed source also said that one of Charlie's girlfriends had told her that his ambition in life was to "kill a cop". (Portrait, 1)

The notion that Charlie had previously considered suicide is backed up by comments recorded in the police report. John Risner told police that Simpson was depressed most of the time and had "mentioned to him about committing suicide as there was nothing for him to live for." Jim Thompson, who police considered a leader of the hippie group, also told police that Simpson had mentioned suicide to him.

The act of suicide aside, both Risner and Thompson were very clear that Simpson had never discussed becoming violent. They each remembered that he was frustrated about the war in Vietnam and about street people being pushed around, but he had never mentioned violence as the answer to those issues. In the police report, Honley and Risner are adamant that what Simpson did was "his own plan and no one else knew about it, he just suddenly lost his mind." (State Police Report)

Representatives from the city had no idea why Simpson took the action he did. Mayor Raine said, "I think he just went berserk". Sheriff Gough, from his hospital bed remembered his interaction with Simpson just that morning when the gunman bailed his friends out of jail, "He was belligerent, trying to pick a fight. But I think the shooting just happened. It wasn't planned or anything." (Burials, 6)

When asked about motive, Sheriff Gough said,

I try to understand it, I think he had a grudge against all law enforcement officers. I think if I hadn't stepped outside and run into him, he would have gone into the (sheriff's) office and killed everyone there. I think I spoiled his plans when I stepped outside. (Floyd)

In addition to considering motives for why Charlie Simpson took these actions, the reader should also be aware that many locals felt that Simpson's motive was tied to a much broader conspiracy. Several conspiracy theories flooded through town after the shooting.

Conspiracy rumors discussed in the coffee shops and taverns included:

1. The hippies drew straws to see which one of them would hold the gun and kill the officers.
2. The shootings were directed by a national hippie organization and Charlie was simply taking orders from this national agency.
3. There was a local hit list that the hippies were working from. Reportedly, G.M. Allen was the number one name on the list.
4. The hippies were working for a nationwide drug ring that wanted to turn Harrisonville into a major distribution hub for illegal drugs.
5. The hippies were teaming up with a local motorcycle gang who would be sending their members to support the hippies.

Multiple law enforcement agencies including the FBI, the Missouri State Police and the local police investigated all these theories but could find no evidence of the existence of any "conspiracy". Each of those agencies' final reports determined that Charlie Simpson acted alone and that nobody else assisted him in committing the murders. The results of these investigations did not stop many residents from continuing to believe in these theories.

The Immediate Aftermath

"No Comment," is what Tim Raine heard his father, Mayor M.O. Raine, say into the phone after answering the call that came in as they sat down to dinner that Friday evening. "That was *The New York Times*, something has happened on the square. I have to go." His father grabbed his keys and quickly went out the door. An hour or two later, he called his wife, Mary Lou, and told her to pack a bag for her and the kids. They were going to go and stay with a relative for a few days. The mayor had heard rumors of death threats to himself and other local leaders, and he wanted to ensure that his family would be safe.

As soon as the shooting stopped, the square became a beehive of activity. Paramedics arrived to deal with the dead and wounded, and law enforcement swarmed all over the crime scene. All traffic into the square was blocked and the people who had just happened to be on the square all flocked to different points of interest to try and figure out what had just happened. According to the police report, Officer Marler was pronounced dead on arrival at the hospital. His body had "three and possibly five bullet wounds." (State Police, 3) Even though eyewitnesses report that Officer Wirt was dead as he lay on the sidewalk, the police report says that Officer Wirt died shortly after arrival at the hospital, his body containing "four and possibly five bullet wounds." (State Police, 3) Dr. Robert Henry who examined all the bodies clarified that Officer Marler had two wounds in the chest, two in the stomach, and one in each hand. Officer Wirt was shot twice in the stomach and three times in his right arm. (Butler, Gun Spree, 1)

Charlie Simpson was pronounced dead on arrival at the Harrisonville Medical Center. Simpson's personal effects included:

An empty Universal 30-caliber Carbine rifle, serial 177729, and an empty 30-round clip, which was found lying near Simpson's body. 368 rounds of live 30-caliber ammunition were found in the jacket pockets of Simpson, three (3) full 30-round clips, one

30-round clip with 29 rounds, one full 15-round clip, and 234 live rounds loose in pockets. (State Police, 3)

Also found on the body was a bank book from Farmers and Commercial Bank, Holden, Missouri. The bank book showed that Simpson had withdrawn $1,550 that morning. Personal items also included a copy of a receipt for ammunition from Hickman Mills Sales Company and a copy of the pamphlets that were to be

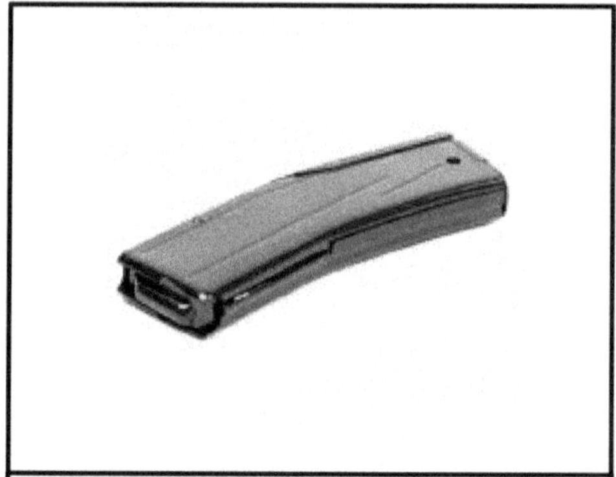

Figure 45: *The above image shows an M-1 30 caliber clip like the ones that Simpson was carrying.*

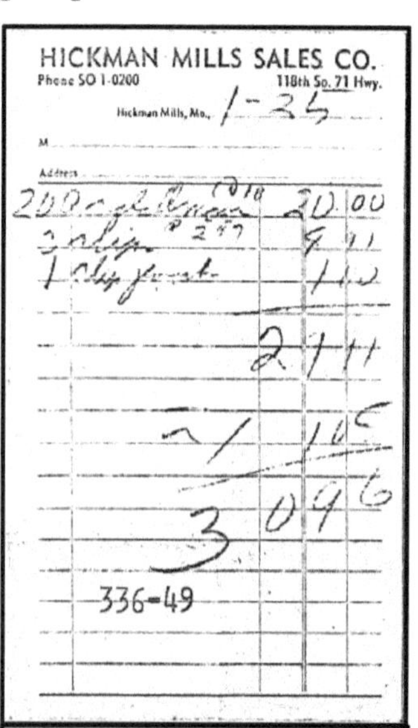

Figure 46: Receipt from Hickman Sales Co. for ammunition and clips

distributed at the protest on the square scheduled for the next day, April 22, 1972.

The square was locked down to prohibit any vehicles, but police did not forbid pedestrians to enter the square. Hearing all the commotion, G.M. Allen ran from his bank to the other side of the square to see what was happening. On his way past the courthouse, he passed Gary Hale, who reportedly yelled, "You satisfied now? You see what you've done?"

"Get out of my way, you little bastard!" retorted G.M. Allen as he hurried to activate the civil defense sirens. (Eszterhas, Charlie, 46)

Mr. Allen immediately put the call out to his volunteer fire department as well as his civil defense force. In minutes, Allen had his men patrolling the square, to assist law enforcement personnel. It is said that many of the volunteers carried whatever weapons they had handy, ranging from fire axes, to shotguns, to Billy clubs. There was also a man posted in the cupola of the courthouse with a rifle responsible for watching the entire scene.

John Risner and Russell Honley, who were in the car that Simpson exited in the alley, said that shortly after Simpson left the car, they heard shots. Frightened by the shots, they drove away from the square heading north on Independence Street. Curiosity quickly got the better of them and they returned to the square with both being seen on the square after the events had unfolded. Risner says that when he arrived, Orville Allen's body and the officer's bodies had been removed, but Charlie's body still lay on the sidewalk in front of the retirement home. Thirteen-year-old, Bob Atkinson, remembers arriving on the scene and witnessing Risner on the street screaming "You killed my brother! You killed my brother" over and over. Atkinson's house was only about two hundred yards from the retirement home.

Bob remembers seeing Simpson's body lying in front of the middle doors of the facility. The body was laying in the doorway with the feet still on the threshold of the door and the head laying closer to the edge of the sidewalk with blood still pooling under his head. He then saw John Risner taking his army fatigue jacket off and covering Simpson's head with the garment.

Risner's recollection that Simpson's body was the last to be removed does seem to sync with other accounts that note that the four victims of Simpson's rampage, were removed from the area quickly and taken to the hospital.   To be fair, it should also be noted that at least two, possibly three, of the four victims were still alive when paramedics took them away from the square. Simpson on the other hand was clearly no longer living. Risner, who lived just a few doors west of the jail, on Pearl Street, recalls yelling at Mrs. Ray Stewart, an owner of Capitol Cleaners, when she came out and asked him, "Why did he try to shoot me, Johnny? I didn't do anything to him." In response, Risner yelled, "Shut up, goddamn you, just shut up!" (Eszterhas, Charlie, 46)

It was after dark when the mayor picked up his family and started out of town. Telling his family that he needed to stop by the square before they left town, he pulled up to the barricade on the northeast corner of the square, he rolled down his window, and had a brief conversation with a man in the intersection. Tim remembers his father saying, "just let them stay". Tim is not sure who he was referring to but does remember the square being full of people including first responders, men in suits (FBI?), and what he called armed citizens. The armed citizens he saw were likely the members of G.M. Allen's volunteer fire department and the local Civil Defense volunteers, who were patrolling the square. Rolling up his window, Mayor Raine pulled away and took his family out of town.

At this point, the entire town was crawling with law enforcement, not only on the square but also out patrolling the entrances to the city. The rumor mill was working overtime. Rumors involving armies of hippies coming to avenge Simpson's death, the Black Panthers and all kinds of other wild rumors had the local authorities on high alert. This army of law enforcement officers was stopping anyone coming into town and turning them around if they did not have a good reason to be there. This included anyone from the media.

Why the seemingly "over the top" response? After all, the shooter was already dead. The reason is that, at the time, nobody knew if the event was over or if the event that had already taken place was just the first part of a more elaborate plan the hippies had to cause havoc on the square. As has been mentioned earlier, rumors were flying, and the local authorities had no idea what to expect next. They decided to respond with a "better safe than sorry" approach to protecting the residents of the town.

Reporters were doing everything they could to get on the square and get the facts of the events for the next day's paper. Mayor Raine told one reporter,

Hell, we don't know how to cope with this kind of thing any better than anybody else. We don't want to harass these kids. We just want them to behave when they come to town and respect other person's rights. (Harrisonville Ponders)

After a quick meeting, the mayor and town council enacted a town curfew which required residents to stay indoors from 6 pm to 6 am, justifying the curfew by saying, "Emotions were running high. We put the curfew on to protect the citizens. We just wanted everyone inside and off the streets." (City Lifts Curfew) By 11 pm on that Friday night, a thunderstorm rolled into town and the scene of the crime was largely deserted.

The significant law enforcement presence was back the next day. Due to the large number of officers in town, the hippies wisely decide to make themselves scarce and stay off the square. The anti-war protest was canceled as was the fire truck parade. John Risner is quoted as saying,

There was blood in those people's eyes. It was like we'd all pulled the trigger, not just Ootney. They couldn't do anything to Ootney because he was smart and blew his brains out, but we're still here. I was really scared. Those people were crazy. The pigs were looking at us like they could hardly wait to tickle their triggers. We knew that if any of us, like, made the smallest wrong move, one of us would be dead and they'd just make up some bogosity and get away with calling it justified murder. (Eszterhas, Charlie, 49)

Harrisonville was packed the day after the shooting. It seemed that everyone within 100 miles wanted to come and see the spots where the shootings occurred. The curfew would remain in effect until it was lifted on Tuesday, April 25th, four days after the shooting. During those four days, the square and city continued to be a place of police occupation. More than one person that I interviewed described the city as being under martial law during this time. Alderman Luke Scavuzzo summed up the fear in town by saying, "We didn't know what might happen after the shooting. Right after the killings, two kids came running onto the square yelling, 'The revolution's on!'" (Wilks, 1)

Several key local figures are quoted in various articles about what precipitated the events on the square. Sheriff Gough from his hospital bed described the situation this way,

I got lots of calls from ladies and girls who said they were afraid to walk around the town square with all these kids hanging around. I've heard they blocked traffic on the sidewalks and swore at people, but I never observed such activities. Until Thursday night (incident at Sears Store) I don't think there was any violence at all. I figured it was leading to a major problem, but I was hoping it would cool off. (Butler, Discord, 2A)

Police Chief William Davis is quoted saying,

They [merchants and citizens] don't like the kids up there and they have pressured us into doing something about it. They are who we work for. We've had lots of complaints in the last year about the kids, yelling obscenities and performing lewd acts in public, but I've never witnessed any myself. We've been in the middle." (Butler, Discord, 3A)

Chief Davis contradicted one reporter who asked about the hippie "kids" by saying, "They're not clean-cut American boys, you know. They're not even boys. Some are 25 years old." Cass County prosecutor, Don Whitcraft, described Simpson this way,

He was a revolutionary with a hatred toward law enforcement in all its forms. It is rumored that had been on drugs for some time, and this killing may have been the product of a 'bad trip'. We have no evidence he took drugs on Friday, however. (Youth Kills Two, 43)

The media focus on Harrisonville immediately after the shootings was intense. Newspapers and news services from all across the country picked up the story and ran different versions of the events in their publications. Keep in mind that at this point, there was very little public information available about the events that took place prior to the shooting. To fill gaps in their stories, the reporters searched for anyone in town that was willing to speak with them. Some of the articles stuck to the facts while other writers put their own spin on the events. Many of the hippies were more than willing to tell their side of the story.

As you might imagine, the reporters who based their articles primarily on information provided by members of team hippie, ended up with stories that painted Harrisonville as a backwoods place with hayseed leadership that was unfair in their treatment of the hippies. It was this unjust treatment that led to murder on the Harrisonville Square. Hippie George Russell told one reporter,

These people have fabricated rumors until this happened. There are two types of law enforcement here, one for the common citizen and one for us. That's the point we've been telling our parents and teachers for a long time.

Russell continued by telling a story about being stopped by a local police officer who told him, "Any time you are ready to have it out, we'll meet you on the street." (Butler, Discord, 3A)

According to Russell, incidents such as this with the local police were the ". . . reason we stick together . . . we're afraid to walk around alone." When asked why their brother and son had committed this act in Harrisonville, Bub, and Charlie's father, Ike, both agreed that

Harrisonville was just where it happened, "it could just as easily have happened in Holden, Kingsville, Warrensburg, or Clinton." (Butler, Discord, 3A)

As one can imagine, these "pro-hippie" articles did not go over well with town leadership or with the citizenry who had lived through months of dealing with the hippies and their antics on the square. The media became the enemy, and it became even more difficult for local or national writers to get information from anyone in town. Of course, like any story, there is always someone who wants to see their name in print or on television and is thus willing to talk in order to get those few minutes of fame. This lack of information meant that the media, who wanted to finish their stories, ended up speaking with individuals who were only repeating what they had heard through the rumor mill. Most of the people with firsthand knowledge were either not willing to talk, or had been instructed by local leadership to not speak with the press.

Funerals for the two officers occurred three days later in Harrisonville. Early that morning, the city council met in an unplanned meeting to authorize paying for the funeral expenses of both officers. Later that afternoon, Orville Allen, became the fourth victim of Charlie Simpson when he passed away in the hospital from wounds he received during the shooting.

Services for Charlie Simpson were also held on Monday at the Cook-Ward Chapel in Chilhowee. The service was officiated by Reverend Ronald Williams of the Holden First Methodist Church. When asked about the funeral, John Risner said,

There was [sic] a whole lot of people there, I think about half of 'em were pigs because a lot of 'em had cameras. This dude, this minister, like you could tell he wasn't too happy about havin' to bury Ootney. He was just goin' through the motions, like he was the one who got stuck with buryin' a sack of shit. (Eszterhas, *Rolling Stone*, 50)

The service ended with a rendition of "Blowin in the Wind" a famous protest song of the day written by Bob Dylan. *The Kansas City Star* reported that Simpson's long-haired friends, acting as pallbearers, raised their closed fists in silent salute as they carried the casket out the door of the church. The closed fist [a symbol of protest] was returned by many of the youths in the crowd of approximately 130 people that were in attendance. When asked about the hippies raising their fists, Risner responded,

We gave the power fist 'cause we figured that would be a way of showin' everyone that Ootney was a brother. No matter what kind of shit they were sayin' about him. He was one of us. We did it 'cause we loved him. (Butler, Man Becomes)

Figure 47: Drawing showing the hippies, acting as pallbearers raising their fists while exiting the church with Simpson's coffin. (Commissioned work)

On Tuesday, four days after the shooting, Mayor Raine and the City Council canceled the curfew. Police continued to maintain a significant presence on the square. When the curfew was lifted, Mayor Raine told the media,

I hope this will quiet them down. Maybe they've gotten some message from all of this. I hope it will make them stop and think. It could have been them, or their brother or sister or parents." (Fourth Death, 3)

The next day, a group of concerned citizens, local authorities, and a small group of hippies met in the basement of First Christian Church. For the city, Aldermen Scavuzzo and Hacker, and city administrator Stephen Berley were in attendance. John Risner, Edwin Allen, John Thompson, and Gary Hale attended representing the hippies. (The *St. Joseph News* says that "Gary Hall" was one of the attendees, I believe this to have been "Gary Hale" and "Gary Hall" is just a misspelling). (Four Harrisonville Youths, *St. Joseph News*)

The city representatives spoke about the hippies' vulgar language, urinating in the bushes, sex in cars, and blocking access to businesses on the square. The aldermen suggested that hippies should congregate somewhere other than the square. The notion that they should leave the square did not sit well with the hippies. Edwin Allen protested, "That's being discriminatory! If we want to be there, we have a God-Given right." Allen also claimed that anyone complaining about the hippies being bad for business was being, "discriminatory." Alderman Hacker told the hippies, "If all of you were working you might have time to relate these experiences that are troublesome and not right. Why don't you have a job?" (Four Harrisonville Youths, 1)

City Administrator Berley asked the hippies for cooperation, If you would just tell your other friends, we would appreciate holding down on the cussing so that so many people won't hear it, hold down on the petting and the other things, then we'll talk to the council and see what we can do. (Dye, 4)

Hacker continued by telling those gathered that the police were not going to stop patrolling the square. However, he did leave room for compromise by suggesting that the city would speak to the police and "tell them not to be so hard." For their part, the hippies provided a note of compromise when John Risner said, "We'll just spread more love than hate from now on.". The group also agreed to meet again the next Friday to continue their discussion.

Foreshadowing things to come from the west coast, *The San Francisco Chronicle* published an article just days after the shooting that almost seems as if they are trying to stir up additional conflict in the small Missouri town. The *Chronicle* article is the only one that refers to the Harrisonville hippies as "street people", and definitely takes a "pro-street people" stance in their reporting of the events in Harrisonville. The unnamed *Chronicle* writer quotes an unnamed alderman describing the hippies on the square by saying, "All they do out there is have orgies." They quote an unidentified street person as saying, "I have the feeling anyone with long hair standing around has a good chance of getting shot." And yet another saying, "I expect to see the courthouse or school burn down."

The *Chronicle* sums up the relationship between the two sides by quoting an unnamed hippie as saying, "A cop came up to me this morning and said, 'You got two of ours, now we're going to get you. You've had your fun, now we'll have ours.'" (Terror, 1) It is important to note that the only place this quote exists is in pieces written by writers from *The San Francisco Chronicle*. I'm not saying this quote is not true, however, it does seem odd that no other media outlet used a juicy comment like this in their reporting.

The Victims

It is only fitting when discussing the events from April 1972, to spend considerable time paying tribute to the victims of those events. Despite all the social calamity that occurred before and after the shooting, the most important outcome of the event was that three families lost fathers, brothers, and sons to a senseless act. Three men went to work that day thinking it would be a normal day. None of them came home.

It is possible that the two officers, Marler and Wirt, were not personally targeted, but just happened to be the two officers walking the square when Simpson went by in the car. Obviously, the chances of Officers Wirt and Marler being involved in a shooting were significantly higher due to their occupations; however, working for the Harrisonville Police Department would not be considered a "dangerous" job.

Orville Allen, on the other hand, was simply in the wrong place at the wrong time. His murder is perhaps the most difficult to accept as one would not generally consider running a cleaning shop to be a particularly hazardous occupation. Any talk of which side was right and wrong concerning the events before and after the shooting pale in importance to remembering and honoring the men who died on that fateful day.

Orville (Jug) Allen was born in Garden City on February 26, 1914, and spent most of his life in the

Figure 48: Orville "Jug" Allen (Photo courtesy of Cass County Historical Society)

Garden City area. Orville and his wife, June Smith, were married in 1940 before the beginning of World War II. After working at a defense plant during the war, Orville and June opened Allen Cleaners in their hometown of Garden City in 1946. Eventually, Allen Cleaners would expand to Allen Cleaners and Beauty Shop. Together, they would operate the shop for 27 years.

Figure 49: (Left) Image of a very young Orville Allen, likely taken around 1930. (Middle) 1960 Advertisement for Allen Cleaners in The Garden City views. (Right) Orville in his Garden City Cleaners Shop, photo likely taken in the 1950s. (Photos Courtesy of the Allen Family)

Lifelong members of the Garden City United Methodist Church, Orville and June had four children: two boys, Ronald, and Douglas, and two girls, Sharon, and Linda. At the time of the shooting, Orville was working as the manager at Dorothy's Laundry in Grandview, while his wife managed the shop in Garden City. Orville regularly took items from Harrisonville and Garden City to Dorothy's because it was a much larger operation and could handle overflow from the two smaller shops. He was just making a regular pickup/drop-off at Capitol Cleaners when he was shot.

As has been mentioned earlier, Orville's two daughters were present on the square when their father was shot but were unaware of the injury to their father until they got back home to Garden City. Orville did not pass away immediately after being shot but eventually succumbed to his wounds four

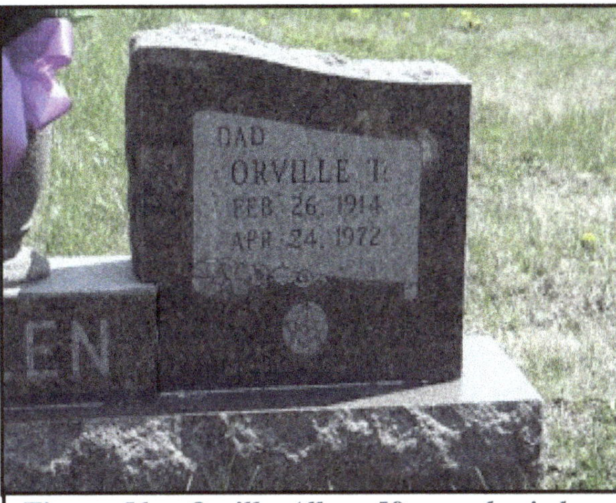

Figure 51: Orville Allen, 58, was buried on April 27, in the Garden City Cemetery.

days later on April 24, 1972. Services were held on April 27th in Garden City at Atkinson-Dickey Funeral Home, with Reverend Alan Pruitt and Reverend Jack Daniel officiating.

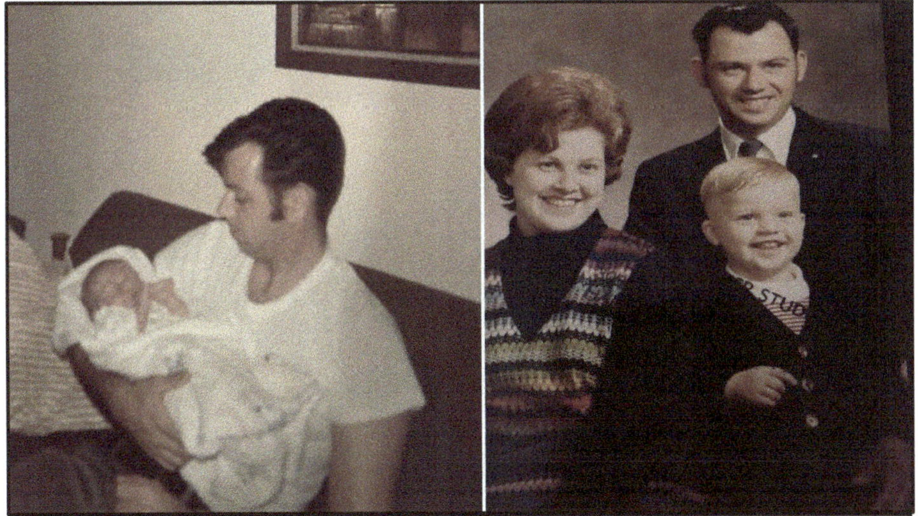

Figure 50: (Left) Donald Marler holding his son, Nathan. (Right) Marler Family (Image courtesy of the Marler family)

Donald Lee Marler, born August 31, 1945, in Kansas City, spent most of his youth in the Garden City/Creighton area of southern Cass County. Donald attended Creighton High School but left after his junior year to join the Navy in September 1962. Don, 6'1", 180 pounds, married his wife, Darlene, in 1964, at the Broadland Presbyterian Church in Kansas City, Missouri. They had their only son Nathan in 1965, while Don was assigned to the aircraft carrier, USS Kearsarge, on which he worked in the fire room. While still in the Navy, Don finished his high school degree and graduated in June of 1968 by attending Long Beach Evening High School and Long Beach City College.

After leaving the Navy in September 1968, the family stayed in Long Beach for a couple of years where Don worked at McDonnell Douglas. His Harrisonville Police application also shows that he was employed for two short stints with the Los Angeles Police Department, one in 1968 and then another in 1970. His widow, Darlene, is not sure why it shows two very short periods with the LAPD but thinks it might have something to do with an injury suffered at the Los Angeles Police Academy, which forced him to drop out of the academy and start again.

Figure 52: Officer Donald L. Marler

In June of 1970, the Marler family moved back to Cass County where he submitted his Harrisonville Police application within three days of arriving back in the area. He was hired within a month and started part-time with the Harrisonville Police on July 25, 1970, moving to full-time on September 1st of that year.

Figure 53: Officer Donald L. Marler's Harrisonville Police ID Card.

Figure 54: Donald Marler was buried on Monday, April 24th, in the Garden City Cemetery

Officer Donald Marler served faithfully for almost two years before being gunned down on the Harrisonville Square on April 21, 1972, at the age of 26. Donald left behind a wife and a two-year-old son. Services for Donald Lee Marler were held Monday morning, April 24th at Our Savior Lutheran Church in Harrisonville with the Reverend W.T. Niermeier officiating. He was buried in the Garden City Cemetery, in Garden City, Missouri.

Francis Wirt was born on October 21, 1947, in St. Louis, Missouri. Known as Frankie to his friends and family, he was the second of five boys born into a military family. His father served throughout most of Frankie's childhood in the US Air Force and the family moved frequently all across the country. Frank, 5'9", 155 pounds, graduated in 1966 from Central High School in Grand Forks, North Dakota. After high school, Frank moved to Missouri to live with his grandmother, who lived on a farm outside of Harrisonville.

While living with his grandmother, he went to college at the Central Missouri State University in Warrensburg and worked part-time at Ament's Filling Station on the corner of Wall and Commercial Streets. He also worked many odd jobs with his uncle, Louis "Bud" Wirt, during this period in his life. These odd jobs included general carpentry, handyman tasks, and painting. He was drafted into the United States

Figure 55: Officer Francis E. Wirt. (Killed in the line of duty on April 21, 1972. (Photo on the left courtesy of the Wirt family)

Marines in 1969 and served most of his tour in California. United States military policy prevented Frank from being deployed to Vietnam since he had two brothers already in Vietnam. Pat was in the Army, and Mike, in the Air Force, were both deployed to Vietnam. Apparently, military leadership decided that two Wirt brothers in combat were enough. Frank would not be sent to the front lines.

Figure 56:   Officer Francis E. Wirt's Harrisonville Police ID Card.

After two years of service in the Marines, Frank was honorably discharged in 1971 and came home to Harrisonville where he again lived with his grandmother. He submitted his application to the Harrisonville Police Department two days after arriving back in Harrisonville in August of 1971. He would not be hired until March of the next year. While waiting for a spot to open with the police he would return to doing odd jobs with his Uncle Bud. In March of 1972, at the age of 24, Frank was hired part-time by the Harrisonville Police

Department, working his first shift on March 25th. Officer Wirt had traded shifts with fellow officer and later Harrisonville Police Chief Norman Schnorf, the day before. If not for the trading of shifts, Frank would likely be alive today. The twenty-four-year-old officer was scheduled to move to full-time on May 1st. Frank Wirt would never go full-time and never collect his first paycheck as he was gunned down by Charlie Simpson on April 21st less than a

Figure 57:   Francis Wirt was buried on Monday, April 24th, in the Orient Cemetery, in Harrisonville, Missouri.

month after he was hired. Services were held for Officer Francis E. Wirt, 24, at Our Lady of Lourdes Catholic Church in Harrisonville on April 24, 1972. Burial was at the Orient Cemetery, in Harrisonville.

In July of 1972, the city announced that a memorial fund that had been established for the two fallen officers had raised over $7,500. Included in those funds were donations made on behalf of Orville Allen whose family had requested that donations be made to the officer's memorial fund at his funeral. The Wirt family asked only for a small plaque to memorialize Francis and for the rest of any money collected to go to the Marler family, specifically for the care and education of Nathan Marler, Donald's two-year-old son.

Help Arrives?

Shortly after the shooting, F. Russell Millin, chairman of the Missouri Law Enforcement Assistance Council, (the LEAC), reached out to Chief Davis and a couple of other aldermen and asked if they wanted his group to come to town and help calm things down with the hippies. According to Millin, "they did request professional help to defuse an obviously explosive situation". (Eszterhas, Charlie, 166) The LEAC is sometimes referred to in other documents as the LEAA. I'm not sure why. I will continue to refer to the organization as the LEAC as that makes more sense given the name of the organization.

On behalf of his organization, Millin asked two Kansas City area doctors to step in and act to ease tensions in Harrisonville. Dr. Jan Roosa was forty-five years old and had a list of credentials a mile long. Eszterhas calls him "Kansas City's most distinguished psychologist". Roosa was tall, good-looking, and generally considered "cool" by the younger people. His partner and good friend Dr. Frank "Gene" Wagner was an Associate Professor of Economics and Social Sciences at the University of Missouri-Kansas City. Wagner, an academic liberal sporting longer hair, had led the first anti-war march in Kansas City nine years before. Eszterhas refers to the duo of Roosa and Wagner as the "Eggheads".

Figure 58: Dr. Jan Roosa. Image was taken much later in life.

The story of the two doctors and their interaction with the town and the hippies comes primarily from two sources. The first is a report titled, "Proposal to Deal with Community Crisis", produced by the duo along with a team from the Law Enforcement Assistance Council as well as a couple of other mental health organizations. This report summarizes much of their work and provides recommendations as to how the town should proceed. The other is Eszterhas' book, ***Charlie Simpson's Apocalypse***, which provides quotes from meetings that the author may or may not have attended. Many of the quotes are likely reconstructed from secondhand accounts of the sessions. It is also worth noting that the official timeline that was submitted by the doctors, in order to get paid for their time, does not exactly line up with the timeline that is presented in Eszterhas' book. This is not surprising as the two sources were independent of each other and created at different times. The specific events and quotes from the various interactions with both sides should be taken with the understanding that Eszterhas' "New Journalism" style was trying to tell a story and there may be embellishment in his writing to make that story more interesting.

Per their timesheet, the doctors came to town and met with the hippies on April 28th, exactly a week after the shooting. This 5-hour meeting likely took place at someone's house or the park since the square remained an unfriendly place for the hippies at that time. Reporting on this first meeting, the doctors talk in detail about how they earned the acceptance of the hippies. Using slang words like "out of sight" and "far out" in addition to talking to the group extensively about their participation in counterculture and the anti-war movement are methods that they used to eventually, in their words, "win over the hippies". Eszterhas reports that one of the hippies kept leaving the room and telling those outside, "Hey man, these guys are far out!" (Eszterhas, Charlie, 167) The doctors note in their report that the meeting started with two young people, "hippies" and ended with twelve.

The hippies did have a set of requirements that they had come up with before they would continue to meet with the doctors, the list included the following:

1. Openness with respect to black—white relations
2. A commitment to the peace movement
3. A knowledge of ecology and the problems of pollution
4. Recognition of the social-economic-political challenges that were taking place in the larger society
5. A reasonable explanation of our reason or "purpose" in being involved in the communities' affairs (Proposal, 6)

During this initial meeting with hippies, Roosa received a call from the sons of Orville Allen. The Allen brothers wanted to come and speak with the hippies and question them as to why their father had been shot. Roosa resisted the idea since it was so early in their process, but the Allen's decided to come anyway. Both accounts report that Win Allen acted as the spokesman for the hippies and spent time talking to the sons of the murdered man. Allen was said to have shown understanding of their concerns and spoke to the grieving men with sincerity. Dr. Wagner told Eszterhas,

I knew then that our hardcore group was not made up of the toughs they were supposed to be. I'd been around gangs in New York who would have looked at those two pathetic guys and said, 'man this is war, fuck off!' But Win was polite to them and said that they were willing to talk. I knew too, that these hippies were kids. I could communicate with them. Shit, these people were just like my students. This is how I make my bread. (Eszterhas, Charlie, 168)

The meeting ended with the generation of a list of "suggestions" that could reduce the tension in the town. The exact list and descriptions of the suggestions are listed below:

1. Jobs without restrictions regarding hairstyle and mode of dress. The community should come to realize that they stereotype all long-haired youth as revolutionaries, indigent and lazy when such is not the case.
2. Businesses, particularly those on the square should realize that it is not the presence of the "long hairs" on the square that is effecting [sic] business as much as it is changes in the economic structure of the community.
3. Training and screening of police. Insistence that the police get to know the "long hairs" and not apply a double standard toward them with respect to enforcement of the law, relative to other members of the community.
4. Schools should overcome the traditional approach to teaching and adopt courses which are more relevant to the age. One quotation by a member of the group was "how can they say that Columbus discovered America when he was met at the beach by Indians." They requested the introduction of courses on

ecology, law, justice, communication …[unreadable] … and economics into the school curriculum. They were quite interested in the techniques whereby a group negotiates for changes in the community.
5. They requested that the police not be armed with riot guns and that they refrain from making threatening comments to the "long hairs." They commented that one of the police sergeants had threatened them with a "shoot-out" on the square.

After this meeting the doctors recorded in their notes, a general comments section that seemed to criticize the hippies for "not being good enough hippies". In this section they denounced the Harrisonville hippies for

1. Being naïve when it came to the current state of the national "radical movement"
2. Lacking a commitment to sustain political effort for bringing about change
3. Being unaware or unwilling to direct their energy and concern to the "formal mechanisms for change including effective political and economic organization
4. Lacking any "sophisticated" political or economic philosophy except a rather rough policy of "anarchy" (Proposal, 8)

The following Monday, May 1st, the doctors met with Mayor Raine and the City Council. Both the book and the report go into detail about how the council also put the doctors through their own acceptance testing, just like the hippies did. Of course, the two sets of criteria were very different. First, the council wanted to be sure that neither of the two doctors were related in any way to the media. The council was very anti-media and would not speak with or work with anybody with a relationship to any media outlets. The mayor's requirements before talking to the men included the following:

1. A commitment to hard work
2. Acceptance of a life's goal and a willingness to work toward that goal
3. A low opinion of federal bureaucracies
4. Respect for "self-made" men
5. A double standard regarding the treatment of women

6.   A patriotic spirit (Proposal, 9)

Throughout their description of the meeting, the writers of the report continually reference how they intellectually bested the mayor and City Council members by using certain mental techniques, as well as never falling into "traps" that the council members would try to lure them. Traps such as agreeing that if the hippies just followed certain rules the situation would improve. The doctors may well have been the most intelligent people in both the hippie and the council meetings, but their report continually references their "outsmarting" of the locals. These boasts are a bit off-putting. The reader should also realize that this report was created for both sides to review as it included potential solutions to the problem. One might question the strategy of insulting the very audiences you are trying to convince to take some action.

By the end of the council meeting, the council, like the hippies, had come up with their own list of suggestions, these are listed below in their original form:

1.   Show regard for other members of the community and not harass them regarding their conservative way of life. "You drive a car, and these damn hippies tell you your [sic] polluting the air."
2.   Not make opportunities for themselves by the use of threats to other members of the community.
3.   Talk to the members of the council or members of the school board not to the young people of the town if the "street people" wished to bring about changes in the town. The mayor stated that he was an easy man to talk to and that the young adults had failed to avail themselves of his office.
4.   The young adults should develop a self-respect, having done this, the responsible citizens would be willing to give them a chance … [unreadable] …not insist upon "starting at the top." At least one member insisted that under no circumstances would he be willing to offer a job to the "gang on the square." He viewed such a move as a sell-out. Others however said that they would provide some of the group with jobs.
5.   Meet the norms of the jobs as defined by the employer; quite a few of the council members insisted that while they did not object to long hair, their customers did and as a result, it was impossible to provide them with jobs if they insisted upon dressing like a "bunch of hippies".

6. Stop blocking traffic in the square, conduct themselves in an orderly fashion, not molest the young girls, and not block the steps to the courthouse. (Proposal, 10)

After two and a half hours, the report says that the council started to change its tune. Roosa attributes this to both the time they wanted to get home, and to his "refusal to be intimidated" by the verbal assaults as to his credentials by the council and the mayor. At this time the council agreed to assign Alderman Felix Hacker, as the council representative to a new Youth Adult Community Council Organization that would be responsible, alongside the doctors, for getting various groups together to discuss issues in the community and come up with constructive ways to solve problems.

The doctor's remarks in the report after this meeting, dwell on the fact that the mayor and council did not feel as if they bore any responsibility for the occurrences on the square. They felt that various persons or groups around the city, such as the mayor, City Council, police, school board, or chamber of commerce were intent on making sure that they were not made the scapegoat for events that took place. They also commented on the tendency of the group to resort to name-calling and finger-pointing both inside their group and outside at other groups. (Proposal, 15)

These comments by the doctors lend at least a little bit of credence to the story from Eszterhas that the meeting was a free for all. The meeting reportedly included Mayor Raine punching city manager Steven Berley in the shoulder and cursing and yelling at the remainder of the council at certain points in the meeting. According to Eszterhas, Wagner had this to say about the meeting with the council,

I sat there and watched them at their table, and I still couldn't believe it. It looked like the Lord's Supper. The mayor was a genuine blowhard. All of them were afraid they'd be somehow scapegoated for what had happened. The whole meeting some kind of surreal melodrama. (Eszterhas, Charlie, 171)

After the meeting, Roosa reports speaking with Police Chief Davis in an attempt to form a bond with him. After some disagreement about whether Abbie Hoffman or National Lampoon were subversive literature, Davis is said to have said, "I figured you weren't going to help us." (Eszterhas, Charlie, 172) It should be noted that later in the process it was discovered that a high school literature teacher had required her students to read some of this "subversive literature" for class. This assignment led to calls for her termination.

It's probable that by reaching out to the hippies, the doctors created an environment where the threat that they felt was reduced. The hippies may have felt empowered by the notion that the city was coming to them for solutions. Within a couple of weeks, the hippies were back to congregating on the square and to many of their old ways. It was as if the shooting never happened. The police were still watching closely but were not actively enforcing some of the new ordinances because they knew that they were now under a microscope and did not want to be the group to which the finger of blame would point.

The first Youth Adult Community Council (YACC) meeting was set to occur on Monday, May 8th at the city hall. When Roosa and Wagner arrived for the meeting, Alderman Felix Hacker was the only one present. None of the hippies had shown up. Roosa panicked and told Wagner to go in and stall Hacker with fishing stories. Meanwhile, Roosa went out to find some hippies. He ended up at Win Allen's house, where Win told him he forgot about the meeting. According to Roosa he had harsh words for Win but eventually got him to round a couple of other hippies and go to the meeting. The purpose of this first meeting was to organize the Youth Adult Community Council. Hacker had prepared a list of possible names to serve on the council. The hippies came empty-handed. The meeting adjourned with a plan for another meeting the next Thursday.

The decision to bring in the doctors, or specialists, to begin talking with the hippies was not a popular one in many segments of the citizenry. Some felt that negotiating with the hippies was like negotiating with terrorists. With that sentiment in mind, local resident, and retired combat Veteran Colonel John Leach, who owned a Service Station and a Gun Shop on South Commercial Street, submitted a letter to be published in *The Cass County Democrat-Missourian*. The article was entitled, "Whose Fault" and laid out the persons Colonel Leach felt were primarily responsible for the situation in which the town found itself. The "fault", his letter said, could be laid entirely at the feet of the 20 – 30-year-old "parasites" on the square, and their parents.

J.W. Brown, the editor of the newspaper, was concerned about printing the article. *The Cass County Democrat-Missourian* was a paper that generally tried to avoid controversy.   For example, the town's paper printed a large article about the shooting the week after the event happened. After that initial article, there was very little news about the shooting or its aftermath. There were small articles about the community meetings, but nothing about the doctors coming to town nor anything about the current state of the hippie situation. Basically, the

Figure 59: Retired Colonel John Alvin Leach, author of "Whose Fault" owned and operated a service station and gun shop (two different buildings) on S. Commercial Street. (Image Courtesy of Tricia Leach)

paper wanted to keep the local civic leaders happy and thus took a very vanilla approach to what it printed. In this instance, Editor Brown went to G.M. Allen and asked his opinion as to whether to print the article. Allen loved the article and not only "approved" it to be printed but also promised that the Harrisonville Chamber of Commerce would pay all costs associated with the printing.

The article was powerful and didn't hold back. The entire text of the original letter can be found in the appendix of this book, but to summarize I have listed a handful of direct quotes from the letter below:

- The young kids looked up to the older hippies, "who thought and acted as they did. Here were the cats with the answers. Here were the cats that thumbed their noses at society."
- The older hippies would "provide the guidance and leadership their parents had failed to give. Play Frisby on the street; that's your right; never mind that you're blocking traffic and depriving others of their right of going about their business."

- As a young person, "You have as much right to do these things as the old men who were here "whittling and spitting". Never mind that those old men worked forty or fifty years and earned their day in the sun. Never mind that they bother no one nor keep anyone from going about their business."

- Why should you work? Your old man has a job and it's his obligation to support you. You didn't ask to be born.

- That leaves us with the parents of the young people of this town. Those 20 to 30-year-old "cats" on the square are parasites. A parasite must feed on its host to survive. Eighty percent of the young people on the square are from Harrisonville and somewhere in the vicinity have parents.

- If these children, yours and mine, were well-behaved, supervised, and disciplined, they would not follow. And, without followers, the parasites would fade away for greener pastures.

- . . . you can bet the minority have let the mayor and City Council know of their opposition to the methods and ordinances that were put into effect. And, in most cases, the people from that minority had their own sons and daughters directly involved with the "In" group on the square. They are blaming the city officials and thereby you and me for trying to keep decency and law-and-order in its bounds. I'm afraid most of the minority that is so vociferous in voicing their opposition are doing so out of a sense of guilt because the city officials and public-at-large are forced to do a job they as parents failed to do.

- It's not only our right but our obligation to ourselves and Harrisonville but most of all to our children to do so. I strongly urge all citizens to write (if only on a postcard) to the city administration voicing our support so that Harrisonville will once again be the town I first knew six years ago. (Whose Fault?)

This letter makes it clear that there was certainly a portion of the town that in no way wanted to "negotiate" with the hippies. Rather, they felt that harsh action should be taken against the hippies and their parents, if necessary, to correct the problem on the square.

The hippies were not sitting idly by as men such as Mr. Leach were writing to the citizens in the local paper. In the files of the Cass County

Historical Society, there is a letter from the hippies to an organization called "The Shelter". I have been unable to uncover any group or publication called the "The Shelter" so I don't know if this letter was ever published. The full text of the letter is available in the appendix of this book titled, "Letter from the Hippies to The Shelter". The letter is obviously the hippies' attempt to tell their side of the story to whatever audience "The Shelter" served. Below are a few excerpts from the letter to give the reader a feel for the tone of the letter as written:

- The ignorance of people in small midwestern towns is almost unbelievable at times. They are so pitifully far behind it hurts.
- The merchants and people who have lived here a long time are so isolated and narrow minded that their imaginations do not extend beyond the city limits. There are a few who have money and naturally they control the city, hire the police, etc. The police who are hired, of course, are ignorant and never question their orders.
- Sgt. Jim Harris is probably one of the main instigators. He has been hassling the freaks here for as long as there have been freaks here. All of the men under him apparently shared his sentiments about men with long hair. Many times, he has told me and many others around that if we want trouble let's have a shoot out and get it over with.
- Myth and rumor, as in all small towns, led the City Council to decide to put foot patrolmen walking around the square armed with guns and riot sticks. They heard we were balling on the courthouse lawn (actually kissing and holding hands), shouting obscenities at old women, and threatening people. All bullshit of course.
- New ordinances pertaining to loitering and people groping into groups of more than three were enacted and town pigs were handed power with no understanding of power. So naturally they started ego tripping, crazed with the power to arrest and neat stuff like that.
- Ootney was a very intelligent man concerned mainly with ecology and literally hated suppression (Authority? Policemen? Violence?) He believed that revolution was needed if there was any hope for mankinds [sic] future existence. He was deeply loved by all of his friends and was always ready to help any person in need. But he apparently felt there was no hope left. But he still lives on in the hearts of his brother[sic] and sisters of the movement.

I don't know where, when, or if this letter ever became public. It seems likely that if it found its way to the historical society's file, it probably became public at some point. The letter is signed by "Friends of Harrisonville".

John Leach's, *Whose Fault?* essay in the local newspaper did not deter the doctors. More YACC meetings were scheduled and a few more citizens showed up to the meeting on May 18th, but only Win Allen showed up on behalf of the hippies. Allen told the crowd that he and his friends were under constant harassment in town, and he was under racial attack daily. He told a story that one shopkeeper was told by a local citizen, "If you sell to that n##ger, we will burn you out." (Eszterhas, Charlie, 175) Win left the meeting vowing that if the town didn't protect his "bros", they would "make war on Harrisonville!" Allen's threat spread like wildfire and rumors were again rampant that the hippies were planning something big in the coming weeks.

To their credit, the doctors did more than just hold meetings, they also met with various government agencies looking for grants and other programs that might help the situation. One of these agencies was the Office of Economic Opportunity, or OEO. The OEO's mission was to assist in job training and creation for economically challenged individuals mostly in rural towns in Missouri. The hope was that the OEO might be able to help the city and the hippies to work together to come up with additional employment opportunities for the young people on the square. The doctors' final report details several existing problems between the OEO and the City Council which led to a very unhealthy and ultimately unsuccessful relationship. The city was supposed to provide a certain amount of financial support which included rent-free office space which they refused to provide. With no office space, the OEO had previously closed its Harrisonville office. Eszterhas quotes Roosa as saying, "I was coming to the conclusion that the people who ran that town didn't want anyone more intelligent than themselves walking their streets." (Eszterhas, Charlie, 175)

Not quite three weeks after the shooting, the Chamber of Commerce presented awards to eight different people to recognize their actions on April 21st and the immediate aftermath. Over 120 people attended the event where they saw awards presented to:

Cass County Sheriff Bill Gough, and his staff; Harrisonville Fire Chief, G.M. Allen, and his department; Harrisonville Police Captain, William Davis and his staff; Harrisonville Civil Defense Director, Melvin Mathes, and his communication

division; Harrisonville Mayor, M.O. Raine, and the Board of Alderman; Sergeant George Hamilton and officers of the Missouri State Highway Patrol; Harrisonville ambulance director, George Van Antwerp, and his staff; hospital administrator, C.W. Meyers and his staff. (Public Services)

Hippies on Trial

By late May, a month after the shootings, the activity on the square had returned to its previous state. The hippies were back on the square as if nothing had happened. There was still tension between the citizens, the police, and the hippies. I can only imagine that there might have been a feeling around town that if you messed with the hippies, what happened to the shooting victims might also happen to you. The police were hesitant to enforce the previously passed ordinances because they had been accused by local and national media of being too hard on the young people on the square. Local officers were caught in the middle. If they enforced the local ordinances, they were too hard on the hippies. If they didn't enforce the ordinances, they risked being seen as rewarding the hippies for the actions of Charlie Simpson on April 21st. The result was that it was almost as if nothing had happened.

On June 1, 1972, Edwin Allen was found not guilty of resisting arrest during the incident at the Sears store in April. At the trial, Sergeant James Harris contended that during the arrest, Allen had struck out at him and kicked him. Sergeant Harris said that the impact from Allen's kicks caused him to be sore for several days afterward. Allen argued that he didn't kick anyone. Magistrate Charles French sided with Allen and ruled that if any contact did occur, it happened after the arrest, not during, thus invalidating the charges. (Harrisonville Man Innocent)

The courtroom was packed on Monday evening, June 6th, for the trial of the eight hippies arrested during the incident at the Sears Store. The small court room was overflowing with a crowd of over 35 onlookers, mostly young people. Members of the overflow crowd had to sit on the floor due to a lack of space for the larger than-expected crowd. Before the trial began, a couple of the defendants were interviewed during which they commented that even though there had been a couple of YACC meetings, the relations between the two groups had not improved since the shootings.

Judge A.J. Anderson heard testimony from both sides with defense attorney Arthur Benson II representing some of the arrestees. Both Don Foster and his father, Lloyd, testified that the incident occurred when a large group of hippies refused to move from in front of the Sears store where they were blocking the entrance. The Fosters also maintained that all of those arrested directed profanity toward them.

The defendants disputed the testimony that they were blocking the door. Attorney Benson called Don Turner, a friend of the hippies and a witness to the event who testified that "Don Foster had driven up and gotten out of his car arrogant and obnoxious". It seemed like he was perturbed, and he started yelling. He told everyone to get off. [leave the sidewalk]" Jim Thompson, brother of arrestees John and Romie Thompson, testified that Don Foster shoved his brother John and threatened to fight. (Six Guilty, 3) Sergeant James Harris testified that when he arrived, a crowd of about 25 hippies were watching as Don Foster and John Thompson were scuffling. Using his nightstick on John Thompson, he broke up the fight between the two men. Harris then arrested eight of the hippies when Lloyd Foster informed him that he wanted to press charges against the young people. Harris testified that John Thompson asked him to arrest Don Foster as well, but he did not do so.

Six of the hippies were found guilty and all were fined $50 for their actions. Three were also placed on probation. Win Allen had already been found innocent of the resisting arrest charge and all charges against Romie Thompson were dropped. Doug Snead had previously pleaded guilty and was not present at the trial. After the verdict, the defendants implied the possibility of an appeal. A few weeks later, four of the men, Gary and Steve Hale, Edwin Allen, and Harry Miller, did file an appeal of their convictions.

Charlie Simpson's father, Ike, attended the trial in support of his son's friends. The elder Simpson who disagreed with the verdict told reporters, "My boy paid the supreme penalty, and it doesn't seem necessary to put these boys in jail." (Six Guilty, 3)

Arrestee/Age	Charge	Bail	Punishment
Win Allen/24	Disturbing the Peace Resisting Arrest	$1,110	$50 for disturbing the peace, probation, resisting arrest charge dropped
Gary Hale/24	Disturbing the Peace	$110	$50 for disturbing the peace
Harry Miller/21	Disturbing the Peace	$110	$50 for disturbing the peace, probation
George Russell/24	Disturbing the Peace	$110	$50 for disturbing the peace
John Thompson/22	Disturbing the Peace	$110	$50 for disturbing the peace, probation
Steve Hale/17	Disturbing the Peace	$110	$50 for disturbing the peace
Doug Snead/17	Disturbing the Peace	$110	pleaded guilty, not at trial
Romie Thompson/17	Disturbing the Peace	$110	charges dropped

Figure 60: Disposition of cases against eight hippies arrested at the Sears Store. (Source Kansas City Times)

The Harrisonville Vigilance Committee

Published accounts differ on the date, but on either Wednesday evening, June 14th, or Thursday evening June 15th, a couple of men were driving around the square in a pickup truck viewing the locations where key events in the shooting occurred. Rob Leach, a 20-year-old Harrisonville graduate, was back home on leave from Vietnam and was cruising the square with his friend and Harrisonville graduate, 28-year-old, Phil Young. Young was an extremely large man standing at 6 foot

Figure 61: (Left) High School photo of Phillip Young and (right) military photo of Rob Leach, the two men involved in the altercation with George Russell on the square on June 14th. (Leach photo courtesy of Tricia Leach)

6 inches and weighing in at 275 pounds. Bob Leach was the youngest son of businessman John Leach, author of the "Whose Fault" letter, that had been printed in *The Cass County Democrat-Missourian* calling out the parents of the local hippies.

The two men were driving around the square so Leach, who had heard all about the shootings, could see where the key events had occurred. A verbal altercation occurred between the two young men in the truck and George Russell, one of the hippies. The altercation escalated and ended with Phil Young striking Russell and knocking out several of his teeth.

A newspaper article that would be written later about the situation in Harrisonville divided the people in Harrisonville into four categories:

1. Hard core: These were leaders of the hippie group, mainly men ages 21 – 27.
2. Long-hairs: These were the mostly teen-aged followers of the hard-core hippies.
3. Short-hairs: This group comprised the majority of the non-hippie citizens. Businessmen, housewives, and "good students".
4. Rednecks (sometimes shortened to "necks": This group was comprised of regular citizens who were willing to personally do something about the situation on the square. This group was divided into those who desired a peaceful resolution to the hippie problem and those who felt that violence was an acceptable answer. (Jones, Vigilantes)

The altercation between the two men in the truck (rednecks) and George Russell (hard-core) resulted in Russell issuing a challenge to Leach and Young to show up on the square on the upcoming Friday to continue the conflict. Eszterhas quotes Russell as saying, "Goddamn you! Come back with your neck friends tomorrow and we'll see who controls the square!" (Eszterhas, Charlie, 188) Like Win Allen's comment about "making war on Harrisonville", Russell's comment worked the "rednecks" into a frenzy. These men were already primed to take action if the opportunity presented itself.

Over 150 men showed up on the square ready for action on Friday night, May 16th. Most of them arrived in pickup trucks and were using those trucks to patrol the square and the surrounding streets, looking for hippies. Others had parked their trucks and were patrolling the area on foot to ensure that the square and the streets around it were free of hippies. There are reports of rifles and shotguns being openly carried by those men walking the square. Numerous eyewitnesses, however, refute that report, at the same time acknowledging that firearms were prevalent inside the trucks that were present around the square.

Anyone these men considered outsiders were targets.   Violent incidents happened. Anyone "long-hairs caught on the square were probably roughed up by the "rednecks". One story has a group of long-haired high school kids driving around the square when they were stopped and told to get off the square. The young hippie's response "We have a right to be here!" earned the driver a beating. He was then shoved back into the car and sent away. Another story is told of a long hair who was caught a few streets off the square. This unfortunate soul was held down while a knife was procured after which a group of men cut his hair down to his scalp. The men then brought the hair back to the square where they waved it around like a scalp. (Eszterhas, Charlie, 188)

Leaders of the group, as well as the local authorities, contend that the violence was limited to a few busted lips and missing teeth. Police Chief Bill Davis said that "some may have got kicked". (Floyd, 2A) There is an unconfirmed story that Win Allen, wanting to see what was going on, peeked around the corner of the square, was spotted, and chased down East Wall Street. While his pursuers never caught him, they did get close enough to snatch the afro wig off his head.   It may surprise readers that there are stories about Mayor Raine having at least a friendly relationship with Win Allen. This possible relationship also might support the unconfirmed story that the mayor offered the hippie bus money to try and get him to leave town, during the height of the trouble. Another unconfirmed report has Mayor Raine telling some of the men patrolling the square concerning Win Allen, "If you catch him, you can do whatever you want, just don't kill him". This quote cannot be confirmed but seems to be in line with a possible relationship between the two men.

Reporters and photographers from *The Kansas City Star* who were sent to Harrisonville to report on the events of that evening and the next were told in no uncertain terms that they would be beaten if they didn't leave immediately. When asked later by reporters about the treatment of *The Kansas City Star* staff members, Chief Davis reportedly smiled when he replied, "Yes, I heard about that, your boys were lucky to get out of here alive." (Jones, Vigilantes, 1)

While most of the rednecks that took control of the square that night were below 30 years old, there were exceptions. John Leach Sr, the father of one of the two men in the truck who participated in the altercation was also there. The elder Leach described the hippies in this way, "They weren't flower children, those bastards were problems before they become hippies." (Floyd, 3) Leach, would ascend to an unelected leadership position within the group. He had this to say about being a leader,

I didn't organize the vigilante group, even though a lot of people think I did, I went up on that square and saw 150 very angry individuals. You couldn't move them; all you could do was control them and keep violence at an acceptable level – if you call a punch in the mouth acceptable. (Floyd, 3)

By midway through the evening, these leaders had named the group: The "Harrisonville Vigilance Committee". John Leach described the role of himself and other leaders of the committee as being the voice of reason to ensure that no one in the crowd let things get out of control. The committee's intention was not to seriously injure anyone. They simply wanted to make sure the hippies, particularly the 10 – 20 "hard core" leaders, were removed from the Harrisonville Square. Leach would later admit, "We realize that this wasn't exactly the American way of doing things. But it was the last resort. We'd tried everything else, and it hadn't worked." (Floyd, 1A)

The "Vigilance Committee" would be back on the square both Saturday and Sunday evenings with the same goal in mind. At the end of those nights, the participants would gather around the square drinking beer and celebrating, making the square "hippie-free". The police response to this gathering on the square was not much of a response at all. Local authorities certainly did not officially condone the actions of the Vigilance Committee, nor did they step in to stop those actions.

After occupying the square Friday, Saturday, and Sunday nights, the leaders of the Vigilance Committee decided that they needed one more night on the square. Plans were made to be on the square Monday night, but this time, the men wanted the merchants and town leaders to be present.   Monday's meeting started as an open meeting on the courthouse steps where the Vigilance Committee is said to have started a chant of "Merchants, Merchants, Merchants" to force the business owners to come out of their shops and participate in the conversation. This tactic worked and after the crowd grew to the point that it was too large; a smaller group was selected to go to the Legion Hall to continue the discussion.

The Vigilance Committee had composed a document that was delivered to the merchants and council members at this impromptu meeting. This letter can be read in its entirety in the appendix titled *"Letter from John Leach and the Vigilance Committee to the local Merchants and the City Council"*. The document informs the town that the committee has resolved the problem for now by chasing the hippies from the square. The letter then goes on to ask the merchants and town leaders to do their part to make sure the problem does not arise again. The Vigilance Committee lists eight "Points of Concern":

1. Problem of juveniles and how they can be handled.
2. Possibilities of curfews, as a method of control.
3. Who has control over the courthouse and yard, streets, and sidewalks?
4. Who calls a grand jury investigation?
5. Drugs. . . Hasn't any evidence been uncovered? Why hasn't some action been taken?
6. How do state patrol, sheriff, and city police work together?
7. What can a private citizen do to show some support for proper and necessary policing activity?
8. Can volunteers be deputized as Auxiliary Police?

Town leaders present at the meeting promised the Vigilance Committee that they would take action and immediately called a special session of the City Council, where they quickly passed several local ordinances to assist the police in managing the situation on the square.

At the special meeting the following ordinances were passed:

1. A new curfew was enacted which forbids anyone 17 or younger to be on the streets between 11 pm and 6 am. There were allowances for returning from work or school activities. The weekend curfew for the same persons was relaxed from 12 am to 6 am. The punishment for not abiding by the curfew could not only lead to a fine for the youth, but also for their parents. Fines started at $5 with amounts going as high as $500 for both parents and kids. Repeat offenders, parents included, could face jail time.
2. Persons of any age were prohibited from loitering on city streets between 12 am and 5 am on weeknights, relaxed from 2 am to 6 am on weekends. It was also illegal to sleep in any vehicle during those same hours. Fines for this offense mirrored curfew offenses at $5 - $500 and possible jail time for repeat offenders.

3. Though not listed as an official ordinance, visitors to the square would be greeted the next day by new signs posted around the courthouse saying, "KEEP OFF the GRASS AND The WALL by Order of the County Court"

Figure 62: Sign posted on the courthouse grounds after the passage of the new ordinances. Also note the bushes along the courthouse walls. These bushes were removed shortly after this image was taken.

The combination of the Vigilance Committee, the new ordinances, and a directive to enforce those ordinances, effectively ended the hippies' time on the square. While a random hippie sighting still occurred now and then, the hippies did not return in large groups. Most of the core hippies made plans to leave town. Concerning the hippies that remained, Mayor Raine said, "A lot of them have seen the light and we're getting along with them." (Floyd, 3) George Russell pressed charges against Phil Young for assault but didn't show up to the hearing and the charges were dropped.

Summarizing the actions of the Vigilance Committee later, Sheriff Bill Gough said:

... the people had enough and put an end to it. There was a gathering of citizens – about 150 of them. They broke up the hanging around on the square. They did some harassing of their own. But I saw no violence. It's been pretty peaceful since the people made their point. When people get enough of anything,

they put an end to it. They've (the hippies) scattered. Some are still here but they don't gather at the courthouse anymore. (Floyd)

County Prosecutor, Donald Whitcraft, was criticized widely, despite urging from many in Harrisonville, for not convening a grand jury to investigate both city corruption, as well as the conspiracy rumors that were still very much alive in the town. Whitcraft said,

There was no conspiracy. The point I tried to make clear was that this case was investigated in depth by 13 FBI agents, the police, the sheriff's office, and the highway patrol. I never saw a case so thoroughly investigated. This was a case of one man going berserk at a time when it looked like a conspiracy. . . . the whole incident was spontaneous and unplanned. (Butler, Book)

Whitcraft suffered a heart attack one month after the shooting. Some in town felt the heart attack was an excuse so that he did not have to investigate and prosecute their preferred conspiracy theory. In an article that appeared ten years later in *The Cass County Democrat-Missourian*, an unnamed FBI investigator who reviewed the FBI file on the shooting said,

There is no proof that Simpson or his group of hangers-on had any kind of backing, communist or otherwise, in their activities. There is no proof that the remaining six "hippies" were involved in a plot to kill or burn once Simpson started shooting. There is no proof that Charles B. Simpson, Jr., was anything but what he appeared to be – a disabled Veteran's son, a dreamer, a loner, a man who today might be called a "good ol' boy" by his friends and a bum by his enemies. (Nichols, 1)

By early July, six weeks after the shootings, and three weeks after the formation of the Vigilance Committee, things had pretty much gone back to normal. The town leaders wanted no more attention, and they desperately wanted the story of the hippies to go away. The hippies that remained in town were behaving and the square was again a pleasant place for citizens to go and transact business. The last thing anyone in Harrisonville wanted at this point was anything that would bring the story back to life. Enter Joe Eszterhas.

The "berserk" Harrisonville hippie story had gone what we would call "viral" today. Newspapers from California to Paris, France, covered the shootings and many of those outlets laid much of the blame on the civic authorities and residents of the "small, backwoods, Missouri town". Many east and west coast readers likely had to check a map to see where Missouri was located. Their disdain for the "middle of the country" residents may have led them to think "what would you expect of those people who choose to live in the middle of the country with cows and chickens in their dirt floor houses?"

While locals might understand those thoughts by non-Midwesterners, it was more difficult for Harrisonville residents to understand this same opinion propagated from Midwest media such as *The Kansas City Star* and *The Kansas City Times*. (At this time in Kansas City, there was a morning, *The Times*, and an evening paper, *The Star*). These local papers were not much kinder to the city of Harrisonville than were the national media. While not labeling Harrisonville as a backwoods village, the Kansas City media did not shy away from the opinion that the Harrisonville authorities caused their mess by not being more understanding and working to resolve the issues with the hippies earlier. In many articles both local and nationwide, these local authorities were blamed for the way they had harassed the young people on the square and pushed them to the point where they had no choice but to take drastic action.

Before being run off the square, the hippies were winning the undeclared media war. This could have been because several members of the hippie group were willing to talk to the media and give their side of the story. John Risner, one of Simpson's closest friends is quoted in several of the local articles and labeled as a "Hippie Spokesman". Local authorities on the other hand would give the media the official version of the facts but little else.

Then the July 6th edition of *Rolling Stone Magazine* was released. In 1972, *Rolling Stone Magazine* was more of a weekly newspaper than a magazine. Their target audience was hip, music-loving, counterculture youth, aka hippies. The magazine designed its content to target that specific audience. The magazine did not cater to "middle-of-nowhere rednecks, who lived in the middle of nowhere."

"The Sad Slayings of Charlie Simpson in Missouri" was a featured article listed on the cover beside an image of Mick Jagger. In the July 6th issue, readers would be treated to articles about the latest Rolling Stones' tour, the legalization of marijuana in Canada, and a feature article on George McGovern, the liberal candidate and the counterculture choice for president in 1972. Advertisements included a full-page ad for "The Toker" the latest in bong technology, as well as ads for stereo equipment, sensual massage books, and the latest albums from a variety of new bands.

The author of the article, Joe Eszterhas, arrived in Harrisonville in mid-May, two weeks after the shooting. By this time, the hippies, minus one, were feeling more comfortable going back to the square. When the writer first parked on the square, he was wearing a coat and tie and his hair was greased and pushed back behind his ears. In the article, he makes a point of mentioning the cigar that he had in his mouth as if the cigar is what distinguished

Figure 63: Rolling Stone Writer Joe Eszterhas.

a hippie from a businessman in 1972. He was greeted on the square by the vision of Win Allen lying motionless, face down on the courthouse steps. After entering Lloyd Foster's South Side Drug Store, Eszterhas attributes this quote to Don Foster, who had apparently been completely fooled by the disguise,

> **See that ni##er boy up there? He's been climbin' those steps every day for four days now and just laying down up there. He goes up there and he looks around and he puts his fists up in the air and then he lays down on top of his face. He pretends he's dead. They say it's a way of rememberin' the crazy hippie that killed our policeman. (Eszterhas, *Rolling Stone*, 52)**

Joe Eszterhas was a 28-year-old, Hungarian-American writer from San Francisco who was working for *Rolling Stone Magazine*. Eszterhas would later become better known in Hollywood for writing screenplays. *Basic Instinct* and *Flashdance* were two of his most successful screenplays. Like most Hollywood screenwriters, he also had multiple failures such as *ShowGirls* that were widely panned by critics.

Eszterhas was part of a journalistic movement in the 1960s and 1970s called "New Journalism". New Journalism is described by Britannica as an:

> **...American literary movement in the 1960s and '70s that pushed the boundaries of traditional journalism and nonfiction writing. The genre combined journalistic research with the techniques of fiction writing in the reporting of stories about real-life events. (Fakazis, 1)**

The techniques used by a writer who wrote in this new style included blurring the lines between fact and fiction. The writer would immerse themselves into the scene which led to regular interactions with the key characters in the story. This interaction often led to the writer developing personal relationships and opinions on the people and events which were part of the story, which could influence how the story is told. A controversial technique of this type of writing is that the author could create dialogue and even characters to help make the story flow better and be easier to read. The logic behind this technique is that while some things are not purely factual, the writer is careful not to change the trajectory of the main story, by their fictional additions. Critics of the writing style argued that "replacing objectivity with subjectivity threatened to undermine the credibility of all journalism". (Fakazis, 1)

Understanding the concept of "New Journalism" and the fact that Eszterhas used this writing style, makes the *Rolling Stone* article and the later book, **Charlie Simpson's Apocalypse** easier to understand. The writer makes his opinions very clear by using derogatory adjectives to describe many of the non-hippies in the story. Specific citizens were described as turtle-headed, dew-lap-necked housewife, corpse-faced, flaccid and watery-eyed, a florid macaw-like spinster, and a flatulent pipe-puffing country gentleman. (Eszterhas, Charlie)

There are also instances where it appears that what Eszterhas writes directly contradicts the police report even though we know that he had access to it as he cites it in the article. One example of this direct contradiction is the previously discussed the issue as to who was driving the car that Charlie Simpson got out of before beginning his shooting spree. The policy report is very clear and quotes several witnesses, including John Risner, that Russell was driving the car from which Simpson leaped out of before the shooting. Why did Eszterhas just ignore that fact? Does he know something the police don't? Or could it have been that Honley was not a character that he wanted in the story. Maybe he felt it was easier for readers to follow if John Risner was driving the car? Another possible instance is when he relates a story about Risner coming out of his jail cell after spending the night incarcerated after the conflict at the Sears store. The problem with this tale is that according to all published accounts and court records, John Risner was not arrested and was not in jail that night. Under the techniques of new journalism, it is very possible that Eszterhas felt that the addition of these small changes to the facts didn't greatly impact the overall story and thus, for the sake of the story, were justified. Of course, looking back on it today, it makes one wonder "where else did he stray from the facts?"

Eszterhas would boast in his book that he came to Harrisonville a few days after the shooting, dressed in coat and tie and with his hair slicked back so he could properly interact with the local authorities. He then would go back to his hotel, mess up his hair and put his jeans on, and go hang out with the hippies. As previously mentioned, the article clearly lines up on the side of the hippies but just about when the reader is about to give up and conclude that it is just an advertisement for the hippies and their way of life, the author will throw something in that takes a negative stance toward what the hippies are doing. In his writing, it is clear that he not only looks down on the redneck city folk, but also has a dim view of these midwestern hippies who are amateurs when compared to the "real hippies" in San Francisco.

The article was long-eight full pages, and approximately 18,000 words. To provide context, a 6 X 9 book with 18,000 words would be roughly 75 pages long. Few, if any, of the 18,000 words were kind to the City of Harrisonville. The city is portrayed as a redneck bastion of idiots who don't understand the problems of the real world. It begins talking about how the biggest thing the town's residents have to worry about is their horses getting stolen by a thief whose plan is to make glue out of them. He paints a picture of a town where cattle are roaming freely in the streets, one block over from the square, and even goes as far as to infer that some of the town's respected leaders have sex with animals by saying that the hippies "were convinced, perhaps from experience that their elders still cornholed cows when they got horny". (Eszterhas, *Rolling Stone*, 46)

The story told in the article is mostly that of the hippies. There are many references to local individuals who had played a part, but most of those references come from secondhand sources, usually stoned or drunk hippies. The drunken state of these sources should lead readers to question the accuracy of some of the statements. It appears that the local authorities didn't really give Eszterhas any more info than they were giving any other reporter. Eszterhas never really tells us when, or if, he revealed himself to local authorities as a *Rolling Stone* writer. I can only guess that it did not take the locals long to figure out which side he was on, as he said that he regularly hung out with the hippies. The fact that he was pro-hippie probably didn't matter much because the town leaders saw him as just another reporter to whom they were going to give as little information as possible. I believe they would easily see through the "hair under the hat" disguise. According to Eszterhas, the hippies told him all kinds of stories about the local players. The stories they told were likely full of nuggets of truth but also significant embellishments of the facts. Keep in mind that he is talking to the drunk and stoned hippies just weeks after the death of their friend. It is human nature that his friends may have added color to certain stories to enhance the image of their now-deceased friend.

Not surprisingly, residents of Harrisonville disliked the article. It painted the town and its leaders in an extremely negative light. The good news for the town was that it was in *Rolling Stone Magazine*, which did not enjoy massive circulation in the area. Furthermore,

Rolling Stone Magazine was targeted toward hippies, which meant that the audience the town authorities felt "mattered" probably never saw the article. The length of the article likely also meant that not many readers, from either side, read the whole thing. All that said, it was still a national publication that painted Harrisonville authorities as the villains. Charlie Simpson, on the other hand, was a misunderstood counter-culture hero who was just trying to make the world a better place. Another point for Team Hippie in the media war.

Thanks, But No Thanks

The only mention of the actions of the Vigilance Committee by the doctors comes in the pages of their journals, later printed in Eszterhas's book. Dr. Roosa notes in his journal that he was back in town on Monday and some of the hippies were gathered at Don and Terry Turner's farm. The Turners were friends of the hippies but didn't regularly hang out on the square because they were employed. Roosa characterizes the hippies as scared and looking for a way out. Eszterhas noted that Don and Terry Turner's mother was frightened that the vigilantes would be coming to their door to get her boys and their friends who were at the Turner home over the vigilante weekend. Win Allen reportedly had already left town after a close call on the square over the weekend where he lost his afro wig. George Russell was planning on leaving town and heading south to get a job. An intoxicated John Risner was trying to find an attorney that would take their case. Basically, the core group of the older hippies was dissolving and leaving town. (Eszterhas, Charlie, 198)

The YACC meeting that week was well attended. Members of the Vigilance Committee, their leader, John Leach, and many community members attended due to the events of the past weekend. The meeting was said to be contentious with the two doctors doing their best to mediate between the two sides. Roosa says that the meeting quickly devolved into charges and counter-charges about the weekend's events. Eventually, most of the young people walked out of the meeting because they felt that they were being ganged up on and were either unable or unwilling to engage in the conversation.

The YACC meetings were held weekly, and most were like the previous one, with fairly good participation by the citizens and very little representation from the hippies. At one meeting, Dr. Wagner made a significant tactical blunder when he quoted Mao Tse Tung, a famous communist revolutionary. A letter to the editor of *The Belton Star-Herald* had this to say about the doctors, or "outsiders",

Outsiders indeed!   The loudest voice, the most eloquent obfuscation, the most vulgar – and sometimes obscene – long-winded outbursts came from an "outsider". He was present at the behest of certain city councilmen and other influential citizens.   The councilmen and the influentuals [sic] were nowhere around during this meeting.

They sure missed something. Their "outsider," a professor of some reputation from UMKC, quoted Mao Tse Tung as one of the wisest men in history. He used one of Chairman Mao's sayings as a guideline to achieve the desired goals of the community. (Snyder, 1)

After the meeting, Wagner was said to have held court outside the building, preaching to all who would listen regarding the criminality of the Vietnam war, the benefits of communism, and the ridiculousness of Christianity. To say that these views did not go over well with the audience would be an understatement. The letter writer had this to say about the local leaders:

Our councilmen and influential [sic] must be excused. They didn't hear the professor. In an emergency, they accepted the first help that was offered. True to form, however, they dumped the problem in his lap and hastened back to their world of commerce. (Snyder, 1)

Even without the voice of the hippies the meetings continued to be held and produced some community ideas on how to engage the young people. Community-generated ideas included workshops on various "hippie topics" such as ecology, law and order, and civil rights. Other ideas included outreach in the community to foster participation in the YACC, targeting trash pickup as a shared interest between adults (cleanliness) and hippies (ecology), and even a local "head shop" financed by the Small Business Association to provide dress for the "street group". (Proposal, 24) Few, if any, of these ideas ever got off the ground due to a lack of interest by the town's young people. But the doctors kept trying.

Their efforts the last week of June focused on trying to get the young people more involved with the YACC. Win Allen was back in town and Roosa commented that Allen had turned into a roadblock to their efforts because he held a respected position in the group and would constantly change subjects and badmouth the YACC and thus the efforts of the doctors. Roosa had this to say about his talks with the hippies and his efforts to get them to take part in the YACC,

> **Absolutely no attention span on the part of most of them. The rest don't know how to get involved or are afraid. Win can't keep his mind on anything but making it with chicks, and his own ego trips…. I haven't found any way of breaking Win's influence over them and he has consistently stood in the way. He left the last meeting shortly after it started to go home and watch a rock special on TV. (Eszterhas, Charlie, 198)**

The last entry in Roosa's journal is on July 1st. This is not surprising since it is around this time that the two doctors found out that they were not going to get paid for their work during the past month. The director of the LEAC who approved the project had left that role. The new leadership informed the doctors that the city did not want the project to continue and for that reason, it would not be funded. Mayor Raine contended that the project was not approved by LEAC, and without that approval, the city would not pursue its funding. After reading through the paperwork, I believe that the mayor and the City Council were not pleased with the doctors, nor did they see any value in the work they had done so far. Local authorities saw the doctors as largely taking the side of hippies and not being balanced in their view of the situation. In hindsight, the most effective tool the city had to deal with the hippie problem was the "Harrisonville Vigilance Committee."

Even though they were not paid, Roosa and Wagner did contribute to the final report that was produced after their time in Harrisonville came to an end. Both doctors were reportedly considering a lawsuit against the LEAC for their back pay. I have found no evidence that such a suit was ever filed. There appears to be some evidence that Dr. Roosa may have come back to town at least a couple of times. We know for a fact that his long-haired son, who was originally brought in to help "communicate" with the hippies, was present at a YACC-sponsored cleanup day. There is no further mention of Dr. Wagner, who left town in late June to attend the funeral of his father. There is no record of him ever returning to town. The last entry in Dr. Roosa's journal says,

I'm really beginning to dislike hippies. Generally, the talk centers around their wants, their rights, what's wrong with the town, and what a bum rap their getting…They are so sure that only they have the right answer (to everything.) In many ways they are much more conservative than many of the adult members of the community. (Eszterhas, Charlie, 200)

At some point that fall, John Leach, took over the leadership of the YACC, which operated without any funding nor any real support from the city leaders. Over the late summer and early fall, the group organized a "Thank You Harrisonville" event with the purpose of showcasing activities available for young people and thanking the city for the things that had been done since the shooting. Attendance at this event by local leaders was slim to non-existent.

A cleanup day organized by the YACC was the largest success of the organization. The event occurred in late August and over 50 people, young, and old participated in cleaning up several trash-filled eyesores around town. The group collected four truckloads of scrap metal, three truckloads of brush, and hundreds of sacks of debris over two-days. (Two-Day, 1) Harry Miller and Doug Snead, two of the regulars on the square, attended and worked on this project.

While the citizens and hippies of Harrisonville may not see it this way, history seemed to give Roosa and Wagner a big pat on the back for "solving" the "Harrisonville Hippie Problem". In a 1981 article in *Missouri Life Magazine*, writer Patricia Ewing Pace has this to say about the doctor's time in Harrisonville:

Roosa and his longtime friend, Dr. Frank E. Wagner, an economics professor at the University of Missouri-Kansas City, are credited with major roles in averting catastrophe. They organized shouting matches into meetings, persuading the "longhairs" and the "rednecks" to refocus their attention on the causes of the trouble rather than its symptoms. …While the meetings didn't cure the causes of discontent, they did end the threat of further violence. (Pace, 2)

For their part, the city and square merchants wanted to move forward and were taking steps to do so. They formed a new merchant's association called the "Square Center Merchants" and on August 11th published an open letter to residents in *The Cass County Democrat-*

Missourian titled "We Want to be Right". This letter, which can be read in its entirety in the appendix, sent a message to the town that the merchants may have made some mistakes regarding the incidents on the square. The opening paragraph reads,

Maybe some of the happenings reflected on us. Maybe in the years past, we the business people of the square have been complacent. …Everybody has to come to the courthouse sometime, and naturally, they save their shopping to do it all in one trip, we thought. Maybe we let our buildings grow a little old, our stocks of merchandise a little short, but we have been here for years, everybody knows we're here, and will patronize our stores just because we are here. How wrong can we be?

The changing patterns of society proved just how wrong we were. We encountered problems, which have been widely and badly publicized. NOW IT'S GOING TO BE DIFFERENT.

The rest of the letter goes on to talk about upgrades to existing buildings, extending hours, sidewalk sales, and sales tax holidays. The letter ends with this line, "COME AND SEE THE NEW US. WE WANT TO BE RIGHT… WITH EVERYBODY."

Charlie Simpson's Apocalypse is Released

By 1974, the memories and talk about Charlie Simpson and the situation with the hippies had largely faded into history. Sheriff Gough characterizes the feeling of the town this way,

It's still a touchy subject in town, and it's hard to say how folks would react if something like that were to happen again. But the talk is dying down more all the time. It's something we'd like to forget and don't want to happen again. (Butler, Book)

The last thing the residents and civic leaders wanted at this point was anything that would bring the feelings and pain of that period back to the top of everyone's mind. Unfortunately, that is exactly what happened when Harrisonville's friend from *Rolling Stone Magazine*, Joe Eszterhas, released **Charlie Simpson's Apocalypse** through Random House Publishing. The official release date of the book was January 1, 1973, which is surprisingly quick since Eszterhas himself says that he was back in Harrisonville to research the book on election day in November 1972. It is possible that the book was not widely released on that date as I have found certain sources, like Amazon, that lists the release date as January 1, 1974. It was obviously released somewhere in 1973 as there were several reviews of the book during that year.

Upon returning to town to do more research Eszterhas tells of being snubbed by most of the city officials in Harrisonville. He tells stories of meetings with Chief Davis, and other City Council members who, while agreeing to meet with him, refused to answer any of his questions. They were willing to let him know that they were not a fan of his *Rolling Stone* article. One Harrisonville resident who was willing to meet with him was John Leach. Leach had been a fan of the *Rolling Stone* article because he believed that the town leadership was a significant part of the problem, and the article did a good job of pointing that out. When asked his impressions of the book, Leach said, "I think Joe took a lot of journalistic freedoms, but I think there are a lot of good things in the book if you read it the right way". (Butler, Book)

The content of the book is a continuation of Eszterhas' earlier *Rolling Stone* article. At the time of the article, written weeks after the shooting, neither the actions of the Vigilance Committee, nor the story of the visiting doctors had occurred yet. The book tells the parts of the story that happened after the magazine article was published.

While total sales numbers are not available, I can only assume that the book, which sold for $5.95 at the time, did well. I make this assumption based on the large number of newspapers in which a review of the book was printed. ***Charlie Simpson's Apocalypse*** was also nominated and named a finalist for a National Book Award, 1975, for Contemporary Affairs.

There were far too many reviews to mention them all here, instead, I have picked out quotes from a sampling of them to provide the reader with a taste of how the book was received. Like anything that gets reviewed, the reviews are mixed with wide-ranging opinions as to the quality of the work. A few examples are below:

Eszterhas still puts a detailed story together. It does not have the poignancy of "In Cold Blood," for he lavishes no concern on Charlie's victims. Rather, Eszterhas examines the killings in search of some community lesson that ought to be there but is not, and in the end, he is left with an empty generational war.

His elders and hippies are equally repellent and equally benighted, the hippies feeling intellectually and morally superior, yet unable to comprehend that every act has its consequences.
--Roy McHugh, *Pittsburgh Press*, 1974

****

Eszterhas has done a remarkable job of researching the facts behind the cornpone war and Simpson's early life. . . One quickly gets the feeling that this book is not about Charlie Simpson or general turmoil as much as it is about Joe Eszterhas. I'm not objecting to those few chapters in which he gives a first-person account of his encounters with the "necks:" and "bros" of Harrisonville—indeed, these prove both enlightening and entertaining.

The culprit is the new journalism, which has been carried to extremes by Rolling Stone, of which Eszterhas is now an editor. Its stylistic trademark might be called "ego assertion" in that there is rarely a line in which the reader cannot find the author's self-congratulatory presence.

Yet at its best, despite his excesses and self-indulgence, Eszterhas' writing is capable of conveying powerful images of saying in a few sentences what it might take a more pedestrian author pages to say. . . There are some important things being said in "Charlie Simpson's Apocalypse". One only wishes that the editors at Random House had been less reluctant to use their red pencils.
--Robert Butler, *The Kansas City Times,* 1974

****

Eszterhas, a senior editor at Rolling Stone, draws no comfortable conclusions. The book is fascinating, depressing, almost morbid, but it is highly recommended.
--*The Burlington Free Press*, 1974

****

The drive of his reportage seems to break down at the end; but his writing is superb and has made this one of the most exciting books I've read in quite some time.
--James Dickerson, *The Baltimore Sun*, 1974

****

… what a theme Eszterhas might have had if he had really paid attention to Harrisonville. He might have found there not only a senseless war, but a senseless war between two equally lost kinds of Americans; the elder, snapping his galluses [suspenders], maybe, but not nostalgic for past liberty and past neighborliness; the young, badly educated, but sharp enough to dig sense out of Henry David Thoreau. I wish Eszterhas had written THAT book.
--Gordon Burnside, *St. Louis Post-Dispatch*, 1974

When the book did finally make it to Harrisonville, the main distribution point was the Harrisonville Book Store, located on the east side of the square and operated by Nancy Bruens, wife of the Superintendent of Schools, Walter Bruens. Mrs. Bruens told *The Kansas City Star's* Robert Butler that she had originally bought ninety copies and those sold out very quickly once word of the book got out. At the time of the interview, the shopkeeper felt like she would likely sell around four to five hundred copies of the book. "It's not such a good book. It's just that the names are so familiar." Bruens also refused to sell the book to children due to the vulgar language. (Butler, Book)

Not surprisingly, the book was widely panned throughout Harrisonville. In his article for *The Star*, Butler said,

> **. . . to make it worse, *Charlie Simpson's Apocalypse* doesn't make much sense to them (local residents). It was written in a flamboyant new journalism style and was full of profanity and talk about sex and drugs. Many locals cite the lack of any research outside of talking to the hippies as a significant flaw in the book. In hindsight, this should not be a surprise since local authorities would not speak with him. That is not to say that the "slant" of the book may have been different if the author had gotten more local cooperation, but we will never know if that would have been the case.**

The following are a sampling of quotes from local figures about the book included in Butler's article in *The Kansas City Star*,

Sheriff Gough:
> **I've heard a lot of unfavorable things about the book. I don't think it was researched enough. The whole story of what happened to me, for instance, had a lot of things wrong with it.**

Juvenile Officer Everett Wade:
> **I was surprised that Random House stooped so low. I was told it was so filthy that most people wouldn't want to read it. It's going to take a long time for this town to get over it [the shooting], and this book doesn't help any. Why, this is the friendliest town in the world. Some will buy it [the book], but most of us resent the things he (Eszterhas) said about the town and the people in it.**

<u>Chief Davis:</u>
> **There's a lot of truth in it and a lot that isn't. I think it ought to be classified as fiction."**

Even Win Allen who was back in town at the time the book came out had an opinion, saying,

> **I'm afraid it's going to jeopardize my family or other black families in town. I'm for letting dead dogs lie.   The way I look at it, all this book is doing is causing people's minds to stir up again. . . people are conversing about it…and it stirs up old emotions. It can cause their blood to boil.**

In late 1974, Elwin "Bub" Simpson, Charlie's brother, filed a lawsuit against Joseph Eszterhas and Random House Publishing in the U.S. District Court in Kansas City, Missouri. In the suit, Simpson charges the defendants with 2 counts of invasion of privacy and one count of libel. Simpson alleged that the book exposed him to "hatred, contempt, shame, and ridicule". He also alleged that certain parts of the book were "false, untrue, fictionalized, distorted, inaccurate and erroneous." Bub's attorney, Phillip L. Waisblum of Kansas City, told *The Kansas City Times* that "Simpson was seeking $1 million in actual damages and $4 million in punitive damages." (Brother, 1)

Simpson's lawsuit against Eszterhas and Random House was not the first "invasion of privacy" case that had been brought against Eszterhas. A prior case against him and his then employer, The Cleveland Plain Dealer, went all the way to the U.S. Supreme Court. A lower court ruling was upheld that awarded $60,000 in damages to an Ohio family who claimed that a story by Eszterhas, which included false and inaccurate statements, had put the family in a bad light.

Through the National Archives, I was able to find the "docket" for Simpson's case (Case # 75-CV-W-3). The docket basically gives a short summary of the case and its resolution. According to the docket, the case was "Dismissed with Prejudice" on July 26th, 1976. When a case is "Dismissed with Prejudice" it means that the case cannot be refiled. Based on the information contained in the docket, it appears that the case was dismissed because the statute of limitation had expired for the case to be filed.

As of 2023, the book has been out of print for many years and is a collector's item. A hardback copy can be purchased on Amazon for around $500. The book has maintained a bit of notoriety in today's literary world as a shining example of the short lived "new journalism". In a review published in the *St. Louis Post-Dispatch* in 2017, writer Chris Orlet says that ***Charlie Simpson's Apocalypse*** "is among the overlooked gems of the influential but short-lived genre known as New Journalism."

Paying Tribute

In remembrance of the two officers killed by Charlie Simpson, the city placed a plaque under the front window of the Allen Bank building. Passersby may have missed it because its location "under the window"

Figure 65: The memorial plaque is now located at eye-level to the right of the Allen Bank Building doorway.

meant that the plaque was only a few inches off the ground and could easily go unnoticed.

The city opened Marler-Wirt Park in May of 1984, at the corner of South Independence and Commercial. The new park was named after the fallen officers and was located at the previous location of George Hoke's Skelly Station. In

Figure 64: Original drawing of Marler-Wirt Memorial Park. Drawing by Carol Burton

1993 the name of the park was changed to Marler-Wirt-Allen Park, to include Orville Allen, who also lost his life that day. The police chief at the time, Norman Schnorf, gave an emotional speech at the renaming ceremony.

Figure 66:   Marler-Wirt-Allen Park is located one block off the square at the corner of W. Mechanic and S. Independence Streets.

In 2012, Harrisonville Police Chief John Hofer decided that he wanted to do more to honor the memory of the two officers who had fallen in the line of duty. With 2012 being the 40th anniversary of the killings, Hofer began to organize a memorial event to recognize the men who had died on that day in 1972. To prepare for the event, Hofer had the memorial plaque moved from below the windows to another spot on the building. The plaque was cleaned and polished and then remounted at eye-level so more people would see it.

The memorial event was held on Saturday, April 21, 2012, forty years to the day after the incident. Fellow officers and families of the deceased men came from across the country to honor their fallen friends and family members. At the ceremony, the badge numbers of Officers Marler and Wirt were officially retired. The officer's badge numbers; #250, Marler, and #245, Wirt, had stopped being used about two years prior when Hofer realized that they were still being used. The ceremony made the retirement of those badges official. The city also unveiled a new decal for its patrol cars at the ceremony. The new decal contained both officer's names as well as the name of Orville Allen, whose name was located below the city logo.

Beginning with the 40th anniversary ceremony, the Harrisonville Police Department began to honor the fallen officers annually, by wearing the French Blue Uniform that Marler and Wirt wore the day that they were killed. (Bradley) The department followed this tradition

Figure 67: New police vehicle decal unveiled at the April 2012 ceremony.

until around 2015, when they stopped wearing the ceremonial uniforms because they were not compatible with the bullet proof vests that the officers began wearing at that time.

Also in 2012, the Harrisonville Police began awarding three annual scholarships, one for each of the men killed. The scholarships, which are funded by payroll deductions from department staff and other city employees, are awarded to high school seniors seeking a career in law enforcement.

In 2022, plans were made for a rededication of Marler-Wirt-Allen Park after major improvements had been made to the park. The rededication was planned for April 21, 2022, 50 years after the events on the square. The event was held at the park, where Harrisonville Mayor Judy Bowman and Randy Jones, grandson of Orville Allen, spoke to the crowd that filled the small but beautifully reimagined park. A reception was held

Figure 68: Harrisonville Mayor Judy Bowman speaks to the crowd at the 2022 rededication of Marler-Wirt-Allen Park.

afterward during which Police Chief Hofer made remarks, followed by Darlene and Nathan Marler who also spoke to the crowd.

Figure 69: Harrisonville Police Chief John Hofer (right) with Officer Dylan Bell (left) and Sergeant Michael Davis (center) speaking at the 2022 reception memorializing the 50th anniversary of the shootings.

Whose Fault?

As John Leach asked in his letter in June of 1972, "Whose Fault" was it? Soon after the shootings and later in time, many of those involved were asked a version of that same question. Some local authorities seemed to believe that if something had been done more quickly, the situation would not have escalated to the point that it did. Sheriff Gough said, "My personal opinion is that it never would have happened if we hadn't let it go so far." G.M. Allen voiced a similar sentiment when asked how the city would handle a comparable situation in the future, answered "We might not let it go so long before trying to put it down. Most people had the idea that if we ignored it, it would go away." (Butler Book)

Edwin Allen, who left Harrisonville after the actions of the Vigilance Committee in June of 1972, came back to town several times in the next couple of years to see his family. According to a *Kansas City Star* report, Allen said that "for the most part I have been left alone, but I still fear for my life." Allen goes on to tell the reporter that if he had to do it all over again, we would probably tone things down a little.

I guess I was into exposing the truth irregardless[sic] of who it might prick. Well, a man's supposed to learn by his mistakes, and I'm supposed to be a rational human being. Personally, yeah, I'd go softer now, I forgot I was black.

In 1974, Win still felt that many of the issues were due to the town's racism while admitting that he often went too far in how he brought attention to this racism.

After a while, when I realized they weren't going to let me forget I was black. I decided I wasn't going to let them forget I was black. So they were after me more than anything. Trouble is, now people still connect me with the whole crux of it. (Butler, Book)

It should be clear that when looking for fault for the events on the Harrisonville Square in 1972, the tragic actions taken by Charlie Simpson are indefensible. There is no justification for taking three innocent lives the way Simpson did on that day in April. The discussion of blame in this chapter, is specifically considering that blame regarding the events that occurred both before and after the actions taken by Charlie Simpson. After researching this story for the past year, one thing is clear, there is plenty of blame to go around on both sides of the issue.

Let us first look at the blame that might be laid at the feet of the local authorities. Both Sheriff Gough and G.M. Allen admitted that authorities should have acted earlier to quell the undesirable actions by the hippies on the square. In any situation of authority, it is always easier to stop behaviors when they first appear as opposed to trying to stop them after the violator has been allowed the freedom to take these actions for a longer period of time.

It is very probable that some of the police and city behaviors toward the group on the square got more vindictive over time. More than one witness told me that Sergeant Harris, in particular, was quite harsh in his treatment of the hippie group. To be fair, other witnesses have related that Sergeant Harris was like that with everyone, not just the hippies. However, I believe it would be unrealistic to think that the rest of the police force didn't at times act harshly toward those in the hippie crowd.

Having spent time as a high-school teacher in a previous life, I have some understanding of this behavior. When a student in one of my classes was regularly causing trouble and forcing me to take time to discipline them individually, my "fuse" for that specific student inevitably became shorter. I believe that the "fuse" for the hippies became short and the police most likely were harder on them than on others. Right or wrong, this is human nature. That does not excuse, "over the top" prejudice against the hippies, but might help us to explain their complaints of being "treated differently".

Several of the hippies came back from Vietnam unsure of their place in the world and not at all appreciated for the risks they had taken during their military service. Rather than trying to work with them to help assimilate back into the society they had left to fight for their country, the town, and the nation, simply expected them to get back on board and act as they had before they left. American society did not understand that something had happened to these young men in the theater of war, and they would never be the same men they were when they left for Vietnam. They were not children anymore and did not want to be told what to do. The hippie movement, which was in full swing when they returned, told them that they did not have to come home and assimilate back into society. American small towns did not recognize that the men that came home had changed and would need to be dealt with in a different manner.

It is probable that Win Allen's racism claims had merit. The same merit they would have had in most of America in 1972. It was a different time. Trying to "fix" racist attitudes would have been monumentally more difficult in 1972 than it would be today. This is not to say that racism is easily resolved today, but again, it was a different time.

The case for blame on the hippies is also clear and easy to understand. Did the young men on the square really expect the local establishment to be okay with the things they were doing around the courthouse? These young people were acting like a spoiled child who was testing to see how far they could push. The hippie culture brought things to small-town America that the residents of those towns had not seen before. Long hair, strange clothing styles, vulgar language and sexual promiscuity were social taboos and unacceptable behavior to the residents of a small midwestern town.

The doctors had it right in their criticism of the Harrisonville hippies in their final report. They noted that the local hippies did not fully understand the concept of how to work within the system to bring about change. In their defense, the Harrisonville hippies were taking their cues from national hippie figures like Jerry Rubin and Abbie Hoffman, not exactly poster boys for helping young people assimilate into polite society.

How would you react today if someone moved in next door that walked around nude every day in places that your family would see them? The point is that the behavior the hippies were displaying was way over the line of what was acceptable at the time. Not only were they acting in ways that were not acceptable to polite society, but they were also throwing this behavior into the face of the society in which they were living. Some sort of retribution should have been expected. Of course, to be fair, one of the main tenets of the hippie culture was to "challenge authority" at every opportunity.

In their desire to be able to do whatever they wanted; the hippies seemed to totally ignore that other people also had individual rights.

The doctors seemed to get it right again when they pointed out that the hippies were convinced that they, and only they, were correct in their beliefs. No one else's thoughts or ideas mattered. What was their end game? Did they expect everyone in Harrisonville to wake up one morning and decide that they were right and join them on the square? The hippies wanted change, but they wanted it all at once, which was not going to happen.

■■■

Former Harrisonville Mayor, M.O. Raine, died on November 12, 1984. Services were held at St. Peter's Episcopal Church in Harrisonville. As the service was in progress, a lone figure entered and sat in the very back of the sanctuary. The lone figure, Win Allen, was also seen hanging back in the trees at Orient Cemetery as Mayor Raine's body was lowered into the earth.

After the services had concluded, family and friends went back to the Raine home for a reception. During the reception, Mary Lou Raine, received a call from Win, during which he expressed his condolences for the loss of her husband.

In the end, the two sides finally came together.

Appendix

Letter in official Harrisonville Police File

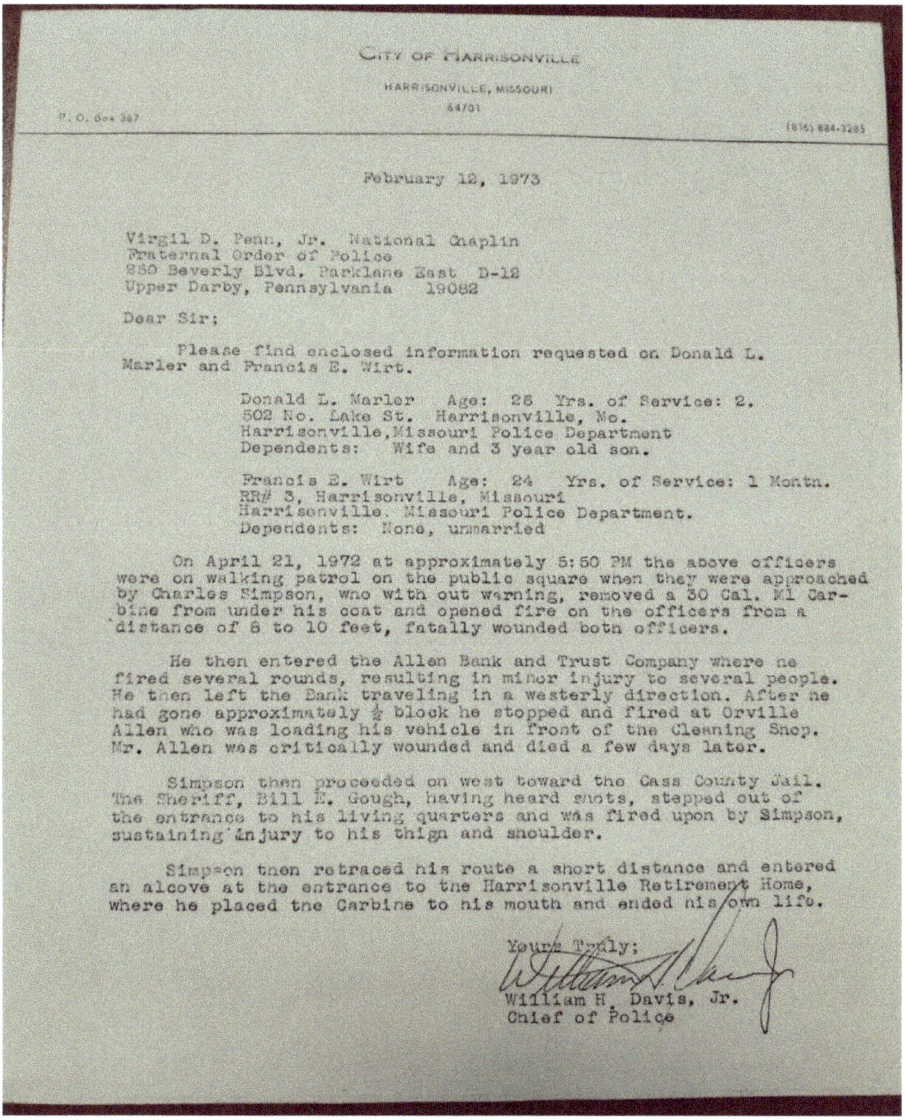

CITY OF HARRISONVILLE

HARRISONVILLE, MISSOURI
64701

P. O. Box 367

(816) 884-3285

February 12, 1973

Virgil D. Penn, Jr. National Chaplin
Fraternal Order of Police
250 Beverly Blvd. Parklane East D-12
Upper Darby, Pennsylvania 19082

Dear Sir;

Please find enclosed information requested on Donald L.
Marler and Francis E. Wirt.

Donald L. Marler   Age: 26 Yrs. of Service: 2.
502 No. Lake St. Harrisonville, Mo.
Harrisonville, Missouri Police Department
Dependents: Wife and 3 year old son.

Francis E. Wirt   Age: 24   Yrs. of Service: 1 Month.
RR# 3, Harrisonville, Missouri
Harrisonville, Missouri Police Department.
Dependents: None, unmarried

On April 21, 1972 at approximately 5:50 PM the above officers
were on walking patrol on the public square when they were approached
by Charles Simpson, who with out warning, removed a 30 Cal. M1 Carbine from under his coat and opened fire on the officers from a
distance of 8 to 10 feet, fatally wounded both officers.

He then entered the Allen Bank and Trust Company where he
fired several rounds, resulting in minor injury to several people.
He then left the Bank traveling in a westerly direction. After he
had gone approximately ½ block he stopped and fired at Orville
Allen who was loading his vehicle in front of the Cleaning Shop.
Mr. Allen was critically wounded and died a few days later.

Simpson then proceeded on west toward the Cass County Jail.
The Sheriff, Bill E. Gough, having heard shots, stepped out of
the entrance to his living quarters and was fired upon by Simpson,
sustaining injury to his thigh and shoulder.

Simpson then retraced his route a short distance and entered
an alcove at the entrance to the Harrisonville Retirement Home,
where he placed the Carbine to his mouth and ended his own life.

Yours Truly:

William H. Davis, Jr.
Chief of Police

Map of Shooting from State Police Report

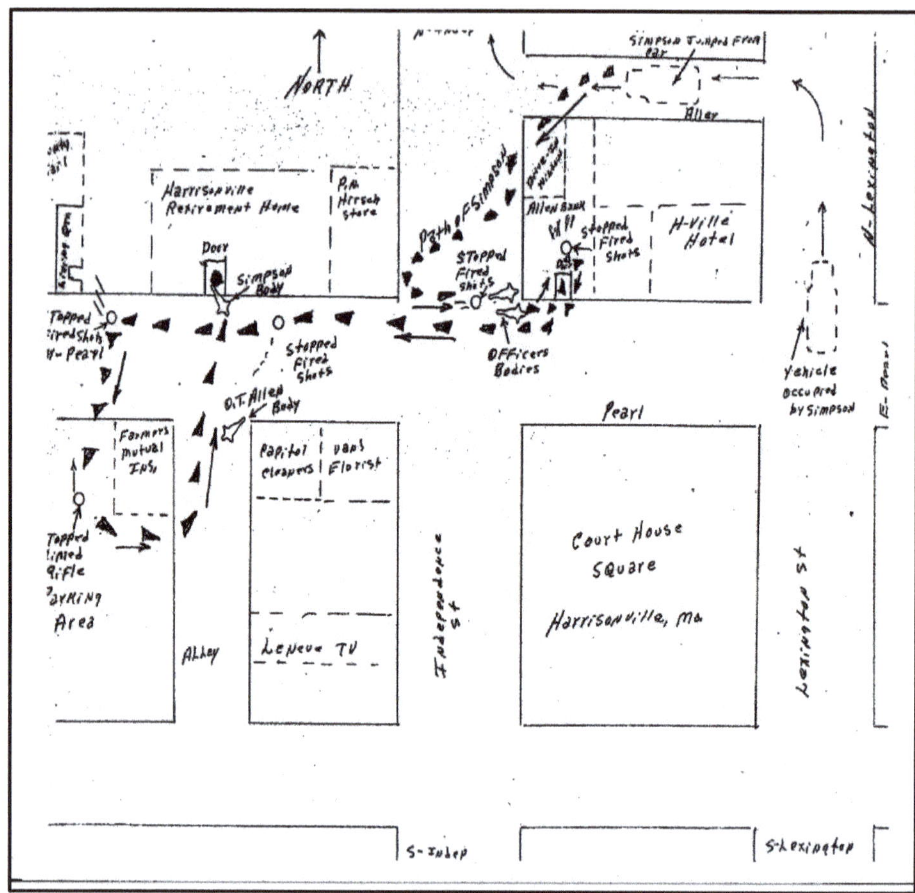

Property Report in State Police Report

PROPERTY RECORD

1. STATUS OR NATURE OF PROPERTY

RECOVERED (HAS BEEN) ☐ STOLEN ☐ LOST
☒ SEIZED FOR EXAMINATION, OR AS EVIDENCE
☐ IMPOUNDED OR RETAINED FOR SAFEKEEPING
☐ MOTOR VEH. INSPECTION STATION SUPPLIES

CRIMINAL DIV. NO.

CASE NO.

TROOP FILE NO. — ACGT20084

2. PLACE WHERE PROPERTY IS BEING (WAS) TAKEN INTO CUSTODY — *HARRISONVILLE, MO., CASS COUNTY*

DATE — *4-21-72*

3. NAME OF PERSON POSSESSING PROPERTY — HIS ADDRESS

4. EXPLANATION OR DETAILS

ARTICLES OBTAINED IN INVESTIGATION OF 3 HOMICIDES, SUICIDE AND ASSAULT, HARRISONVILLE 4-21-72. VICTIMS D.L. MARLER, F.E. WIRT, C.R. SIMPSON AND B.D. GOUGH

5. ITEMS	QUANTITY	ESTIMATED VALUE
Ⓐ 30 CAL. CASINGS, AT BANK	9	.0
Ⓑ 30 CAL. CASINGS, NEAR BODY OF SIMPSON	3	.0
Ⓒ 30 CAL. CASINGS, STEPS OF REST HOME	7	.0
Ⓓ 30 CAL. CASINGS, NEAR BODIES OF POLICE OFFICERS	7	.0
Ⓔ SLUG FROM BODY OF F.E. WIRT	1	.0
Ⓕ SLUG FROM BODY OF D.L. MARLER	1	.0
Ⓖ SLUG FROM BODY OF D.L. MARLER	1	.0
Ⓗ SLUG FROM BOOK SHELF. S.O.	1	.0
Ⓘ SLUG FROM BOOK SHELF, S.O.	1	.0
Ⓙ SLUG FROM FLOOR S.O.	1	.0

6. PLACE WHERE ITEMS WILL BE RETAINED — *TROOP A, EVIDENCE ROOM.*

7. OFFICER'S SIGNATURE — RANK & BADGE — *R.S. Price, Sgt 81*

DISPOSITION OF PROPERTY

8. OFFICER AUTHORIZING RELEASE — BADGE | DATE | 9. OFFICER RELEASING PROPERTY — BADGE | DATE

Property Record Page 2

5. ITEMS (CONTINUED FROM PAGE 1)	QUANTITY	ESTIMATED VALUE
Ⓚ SLUG FROM FLOOR, S.O.	1	.0
Ⓛ SLUG FROM CAR OF O.T. ALLEN *VICTIM*	1	.0
Ⓜ SLUG FROM BANK	1.	.0

Text of Pamphlet #1 found on Simpson's Body

STOP THE WAR

With the Vietnam War now past its tenth year, it is quite clear that the Nixon Administration has no intention of ending it. The time has come for every citizen to exercise his freedom of speech and speak out loudly against the war and all other suppressions in the United States of America. No person who claims to be a human being can justify the napalming and bombing of small children, women, and men. It is quite clear now that the war serves no purpose other than to make wealthy people richer, at the expense of the poor's sons and taxes. American youth have deeply rooted emotions against the bombing and the war. Your tax dollars are paying for the unimaginable expenses of these atrocities, and if you give a damn about your earth, children, and selves, speak out now. STOP THE BOMBING AND THE WAR NOW! (Eszterhas, Charlie, 127)

Text of Pamphlet #2 found on Simpson's Body

POLICE BRUTALITY!
HARRISONVILLE POLICE UNFAIR TO AREA YOUTH!

Discrimination in any form is immoral and unconstitutional. But the absurdity in which the Harrisonville Police Department is exercising its powers is inhumane, unfair, biased, and cruel. The town merchants of Harrisonville act as if they are the only ones paying taxes in the city. They have total control of the Harrisonville Police Department and are forcing them to discriminate against all youth. A town merchant started a fight with a young man on the square, the police came and immediately started clubbing the young man, tightly handcuffed him, and arrested him while the merchant was allowed to go free. Several other youths were arrested and beaten by the Harrisonville Police Department who do not have the intelligence to understand the constitutional rights of the people and especially public property. You are urged to go to city hall, read the new ordinances passed and reprimand the City Council strongly.

These ordinances are in strong conflict with the Constitutional Rights of all citizens and are aimed at and enforced on only a certain group. This is not fair, and the Harrisonville Police Department does not have the intelligence to know what they are doing. As a concerned citizen, you should protest these ordinances now. They concern your children and their physical safety. ACT NOW! (Eszterhas, Charlie, 128)

Full Text of Letter from John Leach
Printed in *The Cass County Democrat-Missourian* on May 12, 1972

The letter below is the full text of the letter written by Retired Colonel John Leach to *The Cass County Democrat-Missourian.*

J.W. Brown, editor of the paper, was unsure about printing the letter. He reached out to G.M Allen, who, after reading the letter, called Leach a "Patriot" and told Brown that the Chamber of Commerce would pay for printing the letter. The text is the complete letter, in its original form, no changes to the content of the letter were made.

Whose Fault?

I discovered Harrisonville in the spring of 1967. After twelve moves in as many years, this seemed to be the ideal town to settle in on my retirement. It had a small-town atmosphere where everyone was friendly and newcomers to the community were welcome. It had a good school system and a selection of businesses that would fulfill most needs. Young people gathered on the square and went to the drugstores for Cokes. The city law enforcement officers knew most of the young people by name and on many occasions advised and helped them.

The "Youth and Civic Center" was open and there was usually a dance on Friday or Saturday night. In the summer, the city swimming pool was usually full, and the tennis court had its enthusiasts. The drive-in theater was a nice cool respite after a hard day in the hot sun. O yes, Harrisonville had its share of problems that are common to small towns. The young boys would sneak a six-pack and occasionally get a ticket for speeding. Once in a while a school window would get broken, but all in all, it was an excellent place to raise a family.

Times were good. The majority of the breadwinners had jobs. Many worked in Kansas City. Wages were good. Even though a few in Harrisonville were on welfare, the vast majority were living "good". The elders had their cocktail parties, golf courses, bridge clubs and a steady income. The young people got the family car and "fiver" whenever they needed it. In many cases, they got their own car. O yes, a few worked and bought their own. They could run the streets and stay out late as long as their activities didn't interfere with the parents' social events.   They were still good, young people but without parental supervision or guidance.

In many cases, the parents were completely oblivious of what, where, and when their children were doing or had done. Into this blasé' society moved a few "hard-core" extremists. No longer juveniles but adults. Young men and in some cases women who had been out in the world and met headon[sic] the realities of life and could not relate with them. Young people who turned inward on themselves and became parasites on society. To these, our young people turned for a lack of concern by their elders. These were the "In" people. Man, they had seen the elephant, they knew where it was at. They promised new heights of delight, a way to beat the system. In addition, our news media played an important part in their development. These young people were bombarded with war, poverty, drugs, equal rights, and civil liberties.

Now, for all the indifference of their parents, they had a cause, a direction, and a purpose. They were the children of tomorrow. Never mind that yesterday the elder generation were the children of tomorrow. Never mind that tomorrow they would be yesterday's children. Their problems (war, poverty, equal rights, civil liberties) were unique. What was the Second World War compared to Vietnam? What was the depression compared to the hungry child on the cover of Life? What was the race riots of the thirties and forties compared to Detroit? What was arrested and held on suspicion, compared to being "Busted" for possession of "Mary Jane". Oh yes, their problems were unique—they had only been through it once while their elders had made the scene two or three times.

But, here on the Harrisonville Square was where it was at, man! Here were elders, who thought and acted as they did. Here were the cats with the answers. Here were the cats that thumbed their noses at society. They would provide the kicks, no longer derived from the drive-in, the teen dances, or the Friday night date. They would provide the guidance and leadership their parents had failed to give. Play Frisby[sic] on the street; that's your right; never mind that you're blocking traffic and depriving others of their right of going about their business. Have a pine-cone fight around the town square. So what if you hit an old lady! Who ever heard of an old lady being killed with a pine-cone? Drive your cars around the square and park them three abreast. Never mind that the people behind you are trying to get their child to a doctor. Park your "pad on wheels" right beside the court house and turn your stereo to 200 decibels. Never mind that the county court is in session and the county clerk is trying to balance his books. Go ahead and take that pill; never mind the results of your actions. Go ahead and commit lewd or indecent acts at high noon on the court house lawn; never mind that young children as well as other people may be passing. You have as much right to do these things as the old men who were here "whittling and spitting". Never mind that those old men worked forty or fifty years and earned their day in the sun. Never mind that they bother no one nor keep anyone from going about their business.

So, they "hassled" twenty of you for playing Frisby[sic] in the street and completely blocking traffic. Didn't your father "raise hell" with the law enforcement officers? So, they hauled you in for indecent conduct! Didn't the judge find you "not guilty" because there was no law against lewd acts on the court house lawn? So, you had a "bad trip"! Didn't they send you to a Half Way House? So, you parked three abreast; all you had to do was move (only when you were ready of course). So what if you got in trouble; didn't your parents assure the police chief, the City Council, and the mayor that your weren't raised that way; so they know you didn't do anything.

Why should you work? Your old man has a job and it's his obligation to support you. You didn't ask to be born. So now, man, the word is out. . . Harrisonville is the place, man, anything goes! The "fuzz" won't bother you because, baby, when they bother you, they bother town's young.

And, into this situation, steps a young man, an adult who either couldn't or wouldn't cope with reality, who can't stand all this "harassment" his followers, his compatriots, HIS CHILDREN are receiving. The overwhelming brutality, the completely unthinking, uncaring attitude of the common citizens to his and his followers' rights as lords of that square! And in an awful, horrendous, few minutes he takes the lives of three fellow human beings as well as his own. While the blood of those human beings is still flowing, one of those adult kids does a dance of victory.

For three days, Harrisonville is chaos. . .curfew from 6 to 6; businesses closed; people off the streets; law enforcement officers at every corner; news coverage outlining the pressure and harassment that caused these 20- to 30-year-old kids to rebel. In everyone's' minds, the question "Why?" Where does the blame lie? Is it with the permissive society where anything goes? Is it with the city officials and law-enforcement officers who tried to keep some semblance of order so the majority could go about its rightful way? Is it with the parents of the followers of those 20-to 30-year-old parasites?

Society is what the majority make it and the small voice of Harrisonville isn't going to change that. The decisions of our higher courts have assured that the wrongdoer has as many rights, if not more, than the common man on the street. These courts go to great lengths to see that the rights of wrongdoers are upheld. So, in the long run, all our law enforcement officers can do is try to keep some semblance of order. That leaves us with the parents of the young people of this town. Those 20 to 30-year-old "cats" on the square are parasites. A parasite must feed on its host to survive. Eighty percent of the young people on the square are from Harrisonville and somewhere in the vicinity have parents. If these children, yours and mine, were well behaved, supervised, and disciplined, they would not follow. And, without followers, the parasites would fade away for greener pastures. They need these young of ours desperately to feed their egos and to get at us straight through our[out:sic] children because they feel we're to blame for their unique problems.

There are those of you rationalizing as you read this. "Not my children, I've raised them properly." I'll have to agree that the majority have. The majority of us are going our way trying to make a living for our families, trying to better ourselves and our children. Doing the same job day in and day out so our children can go to college and become responsible, contributing members of society. Unfortunately, there are parents in Harrisonville who will not or can not[sic] control their children.

And whose voice is heard above the clamor? Those, who are going their way doing their best to make something of themselves and their children or those parents of the followers? Certainly not the majority because the majority of the young people of this town have not been arrested nor do they cause any more problems than would be expected from that age group.

Have the majority of the citizens of Harrisonville informed the Mayor or the City Council that they are in accord with them on the actions they have taken so that people can go about their business unmolested on the square or anywhere else in this town? Well, you can bet the minority have let the Mayor and City Council know of their opposition to the methods and ordinances that were put into effect. And, in most cases, the people from that minority had their own sons and daughters directly involved with the "In" group on the square. They are blaming the city officials and thereby you and me for trying to keep decency and law-and-order in its bounds. I'm afraid most of the minority that is so vociferous in voicing their opposition are doing so out of a sense of guilt because the city officials and public-at-large are forced to do a job they as parents failed to do.

But if the Mayor and City Council hear only from the minority, what are they to think? I'm concerned that they may mistake the voice of the minority for the voice of you and me, the majority; and conduct the business of the city accordingly. I, myself, believe in Harrisonville and its potential. I believe it is still a good place to raise a family, but unless you and I show our support to our duly elected officials, it may not remain so. Let us assure the Mayor and City Council or anyone else that might be interested that we, the majority, favor law and order, common decency, and approve wholeheartedly the action and the stand they have taken.

It's not only our right but our obligation to ourselves and Harrisonville but most of all to our children to do so. I strongly urge all citizens to write (if only on a postcard) to the city administration voicing our support so that Harrisonville will once again be the town I first knew six years ago.

This letter was written by a Harrisonville businessman. It so aptly sums up the situation in our community that we felt every citizen should have an opportunity to read it with serious consideration.

Letter from Hippies to "Shelter"

This letter is in the files of the Cass County Historical Society. It is obviously written either by the hippies or their representative and is addressed to something called the "Shelter". I have been unable to find any publication or organization that has in the past or currently goes by that name. I'm not sure if this letter was ever published anywhere or if it was just stuck in a file, where it has been for 50 years. The exact date of this document is unknown, but the subject matter of the letter tells us that it was likely between May – June 1972.

The following article was written for the Shelter by some folks from Harrisonville, Missouri describing the atmosphere in that small Missouri town that led to the shooting of police officers and several other persons by Charles Simpson (who then took his own life to end the incident.)

As Jerry Rubin says, "we are everywhere," we are also here in Harrisonville, facing suppression of all forms plus the normal small "amerikan"* town hassles. The hassles have been here for a long time, as they have been everywhere in the world. But about a year ago is when we started questioning and challenging the local "pig" establishment.

[Illegible] when several of us just happened to be here and started partying together and rapping and soon found out most of us shared the same fears about such things as ecology, wars and suppression. The more we rapped, read, and traveled around together, the more we learned about how things were really fucked up. It comes home really hard in small town Missouri.

The ignorance of people in small midwestern towns is almost unbelievable at times. They are so pitifully far behind it hurts. Such is the problem in Harrisonville, a small town of about 5,000 people living 30 miles south of K.C. The merchants and people who have lived here a long time are so isolated and narrow minded that their imaginations do not extend beyond the city limits.

There are a few who have money and naturally they control the city, hire the police, etc. The police who are hired of course, are ignorant and never question their orders.

Sgt. Jim Harris is probably one of the main instigators. He has been hassling the freaks here for as long as there have been freaks here. All of the men under him apparently shared his sentiments about men with long hair. Many times, he has told me and many other around that if we want trouble let's have a shoot out and get it over with. The Harrisonville police dept. has been using the old familiar harassing tactics such as arresting us for disturbing the peace, minors in possession, loitering and "I say so." We had a house here for a while which was put under 24- hour surveillance (which of course they deny).

Recently the town square merchants have been losing business which they attribute to freaks on the street scaring people away. Myth and rumor, as in all small towns, led the City Council to decide to put foot patrolmen walking around the square armed with guns and riot sticks. They heard we were balling on the courthouse lawn (actually kissing and holding hands), shouting obscenities at old women, and threatening people. All bullshit of course.

What the town square merchants fail to recognize is that their prices are a lot higher than the surrounding shopping centers and discount stores and that Kansas City is only a 20-minute drive away on the recently built dual lane highway where people go to shop, get what they want at cheaper prices.

At night, young people would go to the square to meet and rap with their friends. New ordinances pertaining to loitering and people groping into groups of more than three were enacted and town pigs were handed power with no understanding of power. So naturally they started ego tripping, crazed with the power to arrest and neat stuff like that.

First a black dude, who had gotten out of his place, got busted because he refused to leave the town square at the request of Jim Harris (on a Sunday afternoon). The harassment by the foot police got more intense every night. Then one night a bunch of street people happened to be standing on a public sidewalk in front of a closed store and the merchant who owned the store walked up and told us to leave. We asked why and he said that he didn't want us in front of his store. Naturally, we didn't move. He started a fight with one of us. The pigs jumped out of the bushes and Jim Harris clubbed the long hair, hand-cuffed him, and another merchant told the pigs to arrest everybody else standing around. So, they did. We started walking toward the jail and the same black dude that was busted before got poked in the ribs with a billy club. He turned around and told them not to hit him again. Three pigs jumped on him, roughed him up and hand-cuffed him. Eight people were busted while the merchant who started it went free without questioning. Could have been a little prior planning there, huh? We tried to press charges on the merchant, but these were [illegible].

We bailed them out the next morning after an all-night search for money. The bail on all of them, except for the black dude was $110. His was $1,110. I don't think they dig "ni##ers" here. Charles Simpson from Holden, one of our best brothers, paid most of the bail. Then we planned a protest for the next day against the bogus ordinances and the war.

Charles Simpson (Ootney to his friends) then left to go home and get some leaflets typed up and was planning to come back the next day for the protest. Later that evening shots were heard and Ootney had ended the life of a policeman, another man, and had wounded several others before ending his own physical life afterwards. Exactly what prompted him to take this action, only he knew.

Ootney was a very intelligent man concerned mainly with ecology and literally hated suppression (Authority? Policemen? Violence?) He believed that revolution was needed if there was any hope for mankinds [sic] future existence. He was deeply loved by all of his friends and was always ready to help any person in need. But he apparently felt there was no hope left. But he still lives on in the hearts of his brother[sic] and sisters of the movement.

Of course, many long hairs were questioned about this by the FBI. Three of us were busted for suspicion of the latest charge the FBI uses on us all around amerika—conspiracy. It is hard for the man to realize individuality after all these years of government brainwashing.

A couple of weeks after all this happened, several brothers and sisters were in the park at night—off the square—and were surrounded by armed pigs, one with a riot gun over his shoulder. They were told to leave. More hassles. Many of us are under surveillance now. But we gotta keep on anyway. We are still here – we are still together –as we are everywhere.

Friends from Harrisonville

*The writers of this document purposefully used the term "amerikan". According to Merriam Webster, this term is defined as "the fascist or racist aspect of American society". The term was frequently used by hippies in the 1970s to describe the establishment.

Letter from Vigilance Committee to the local merchants and the City Council (Original Text)
Date: June 19, 1972.

Since the tragedy of April 21st in our town, many hours of discussion have been spent by numerous groups of concerned citizens. Public officials, law enforcement officers, and young people have met with men and women to probe for solutions to the problem on the square.

Although the focal point for action has been the square in Harrisonville, many of the "counter culture" groups have gathered here from the outside of our town. So the resulting problems are as much or more county-based as they are town based.

During the past 3 weeks, undesirable groups have begun congregating in ever increasing numbers and causing disturbances. Following the acquittal of Edwin Allen in Magistrate Court on a charge of resisting arrest, many citizens felt justice had not been done. This helped increase the growing resentment caused by the fact that no arrests had been made after the murders of April 21, even though there seemed to be no evidence of conspiracy. (I believe this this is a typo and is meant to say, "even though there seemed to be evidence of conspiracy.")

Last week an altercation on the square occurred between Phillip Young and George Russell which resulted in a challenge to show up Friday night on the square.

A vigilance committee of approximately 150 men gathered on the courthouse premises to challenge the "rights" of the hippies. Again, on Saturday and Sunday, groups in lesser numbers kept watch to discourage the "street people" from gathering.

Now this volunteer committee of citizens, who organized to suppress the filthy conduct in public, when the processes of law appeared inadequate, feels the problem has been cleared up, at least temporarily.

But they want some assurance from public officials and law enforcement officers that alert and active watchfulness will be kept over the situation to prevent a reoccurrence.

Also, they feel that the uptown business and professional people and property owners should now organize themselves to take over their share of responsibility for improving the public image of the central business district.

POINTS OF CONCERN:

1. Problem of juveniles and how they can be handled
2. Possibilities of curfews, as a method of control
3. Who has control over courthouse yard, streets, and sidewalks?
4. Who calls a grand jury investigation?
5. Drugs. . . Hasn't any evidence been uncovered? Why hasn't some action been taken?
6. How do state patrol, sheriff and city police work together?
7. What can a provide citizen do to show some support for the proper and necessary policing activity?
8. Can volunteers be deputized as Auxiliary Policy?

Letter to Residents from Square Merchants (Original Text)
Published in *The Cass County Democrat-Missourian*
Date: October 11, 1972

WE WANT TO BE RIGHT!

Conditions and events surrounding the square in Harrisonville for some time past indicate that somewhere along the way somebody was wrong. Maybe some of the happenings reflected on us. Maybe in years past, we business people of the square have been complacent. After all, we're the county seat of a growing and prosperous community. Everybody has to come to the courthouse sometime, and naturally they save their shopping to do it all in one trip, we thought. Maybe we let our buildings grow a little old, our stocks of merchandise a little short, but we have been here for years, everybody knows we're here, and will patronize our stores just because we are here. How wrong can we be?

The changing patterns of society proved just how wrong we were. We encountered problems, which have been widely and badly publicized.

NOW IT'S GOING TO BE DIFFERENT!

We're going to make it FUN to come to the square for any purpose. If you want to visit, fine! We'd love to visit with you. If you wish to shop--come right in. We'll try harder to have what you want. Parking? A program is being worked out to provide ample, immediate parking on the square. Appearance and cleanliness--we're working on that, too. Store hours? We plan to have coordinated night openings regularly for your convenience. Any other suggestions you might have for improvement will be gratefully received.

We want the square to gain a new personality, but it won't happen overnight. After all, the old courthouse has been the center of town since 1844, and some of our buildings are not much younger. But like the businesses that occupy them, they're sound and just need rejuvenating. But the atmosphere and our attitude toward you, our customers, can change immediately. We hope you notice it and hope you will tell us if you do. . . or don't.

A new merchant's associate has been formed for the purpose of making all these good things happen. After a period of self-analysis, we think we see what's needed. A new name will be chosen for our uptown shopping area. Maybe you'll help us name it. At the bottom of this page is a suggestion coupon. Fill it out, return it to any merchant on the square and we'll award a prize to the winning name, Saturday, August 19th.

As an example of our determination to make it FUN, and gainful, for you to shop on the square, we are having two lively retail promotions this month. The first is August 18-19. An OLD-FASHIONED SALE, replete with Gay Ninety costumes, old-fashioned bargains and shades of the thirties, NO SALES TAX! And for the young'uns, a TURTLE RACE at 2:00 o'clock Saturday afternoon with prizes for the speediest turtles. The following week, August 25-26, an old-fashioned SIDE-WALK SALE, with full participation, and real down-to- "concrete" values you'll be sorry if you miss.
COME AND SEE THE NEW US. WE WANT TO BE RIGHT . . . WITH EVERYBODY.

Doctors Calendar April 21 – June 13
Published in the LEAC Report titled "Harrisonville: A Community in Crisis"
Created by: Law Enforcement Assistance Council, Interpersonal Dynamics, and The Greater Kansas City Mental Health Foundation

<u>Chronology of Harrisonville</u>

Friday, April 21:	Killings
Friday, April 28:	Met with Street People (4 hours)
Monday, May 1:	Met with City Council (3 hours)
Tuesday, May 2:	Met with William Smith of LEAA (2 hours)
Friday, May 5	Met with Director of the Missouri Police Academy (2 hours)
Monday, May 8:	Met with Win Allen (handwritten above this line "young black – one of 8 originally arrested) in his cellar and with some of the "street people" and two members of the City Council at the town hall. (6 hours)
Tuesday, May 9:	Met with Doarn of Metropolitan Planning (2 hours)
Thursday, May 11:	Wagner met with members of Harrisonville School Board. (2 ½ hours)
Thursday, May 11:	Roosa met with a few members of youth group on the fringes of the street group. City hall. (3 hours)
Thursday May 18:	Met with group, attended by members of City Council, to young persons and a number of women interested in civic affairs. (3 hours)
Tuesday, May 23:	Wagner met with O.E.O. In Appleton City. (3 hours)
Wednesday, May 24:	Met with members of Greater Kansas City Mental Health Foundation. (2 hours)
Wednesday, May 24:	Attended meeting in Harrisonville, first canceled then re-affirmed. Group included another group which had been holding separate meetings. Church. (3 hours)

Tuesday, May 30:	Attended meeting with Youth-Adult group at American Legion Hall. (3 hours)
Sunday, June 4:	Met with Roosa and Wagner to discuss program. (6 hour)
Tuesday, June 6:	Trip to Harrisonville, 7:30 – 11:30, Roosa, Wagner, and Perusse met with Youth Adult Community Council. (4 hours)
Friday, June 9:	Meeting with Harrisonville students. (1 ½ hours) Meeting with Russ Millin, Roosa, Perusse to discuss Project. (2 hours)
Tuesday, June 13:	Wagner and Perusse meet with Adult Youth Committee – to solicit additional technical assistance from L.E.A.A. [sic] Youth hostile and arming over arrest of young black . . . (end of notes)

Allen, Randall. "Orville Allen." E-mail to the author, 21 Jan. 2023.

"Allen's Cleaners Advertisement." *The Garden City Views* [Garden City], 27 July 1960, p. 5.

"Almanac.com." *Almanac*, Yankee Publishing, www.almanac.com/weather/history/MO/Harrisonville/ 1972-01-26. Accessed 10 Nov. 2022.

Atkinson, Bob. Personal interview with the author. 15 September. 2022.

Atkinson, David. Personal interview with the author. 6 Aug. 2022.

Anonymous, Personal interview with the author. 9 November, 2022.

Beggs, Scott. "10 Revolutionary Facts About Abbie Hoffman." *Mental Floss*, Minute Media, 16 Oct. 2020, www.mentalfloss.com/article/633698/abbie-hoffman-facts. Accessed 7 June 2022.

Bohl, Carol, and David R. Atkinson. *Harrisonville*. Charleston, South Carolina, Arcadia Publishing, 2012. Images of America.

Bradley, Donald. "A hurtful memory." *The Kansas City Star* [Kansas City], 16 Apr. 2012, pp. 1+.

Brosnan, James W. "Six Guilty at Harrisonville." *The Kansas City Times* [Kansas City], 6 June 1972, p. 3.

"Brother Sues Over Book on Simpson." *The Kansas City Times* [Kansas City], 4 Jan.1975.

"Burials echo sheriff's fears." *Jefferson City Post-Tribune* [Jefferson City], 24 Apr. 1972, p. 6.

Burnside, Gordon. "Sad Wars of Lost Americans." *St. Louis Post-Dispatch* [St. Louis], 6 Jan. 1974, p.40.

Butler, Robert W. "Book Brings Back Painful Memories for Harrisonville." *The Kansas City Times* [Kansas City], 10 Jan. 1974, pp. 1+.

Butler, Robert W. "Harrisonville Gun Spree: 3 Dead."*The Kansas City Times* [Kansas City], 22 Apr. 1972, pp. 1-2.

Butler, Robert W. "Man Becomes 4th Victim In Harrisonville Shootings." *Kansas City Star* [Kansas City], 25 Apr. 1972.

Butler, Robert. "That Cornpone War at Harrisonville."*The Kansas City Star* [Kansas City], 6 Jan.   1974, sec. E, p. 93.

Calcagni, Dustin. *Understanding of the Hippies; History of the Hippie Movement up to the Present Day*. 2021.

Campbell, William C., and Jeff Price. "Harrisonville Seeks Reason for Tragedy." *The Kansas City Star* [Kansas City], 23 Apr. 1972, pp. 1-2.

Catron, Doug. Personal interview with the author. 5 September. 2022.

"City Council Sets Curfew Here." *The Cass County Democrat-Missou rian* [Harrisonville], 30 June 1972.

"Chilling 'Apocalypse' Provides No Answers." *The Burlington Free Press*[Burlington], 18 Apr. 1974, Book Reviews sec., p. 16.

Davis, William H. Letter to Darlene Hardy.   17 May 1984, Harrison ville Police Files. Manusc.

Dickerson, James. "Book Review." *The Baltimore Sun* [Baltimore], 13 Jan. 1974, p. 47.

Dye, Robert M. "Town Talks Out Conflict." *The Kansas City Star* [Kansas City], 27 Apr. 1972, p. 4.

"Ex-Harrisonville mayor Dr. M.O. Raine is dead." *The Kansas City Times* [Kansas City], 13 Nov. 1984, p. 34.

"Four Harrisonville Youths Meet with 3 Town Officials." *St. Joseph News-Press* [St. Joseph], 27 Apr. 1972, p. 5.

Eszterhas, Joe. *Charlie Simpson's Apocalypse.* New York City,   Rand om House, 1973.

Eszterhas, Joe. "The Tragic Slaying of Hippie-Freak Charlie Simpson. " *Rolling Stone Magazine*, 6 July 1972, pp. 45-52.

Fakazis, Liz. "New Journalism." *Britannica.com*, Britannica, www.brit annica.com/topic/New-Journalism. Accessed 20 Dec. 2022.

Floyd, James. "Harrisonville, Mo." *St. Louis Globe Democrat*   [St. Louis], 21 Oct. 1972, sec. F.

"Four to Appeal Court Ruling." *The Cass County Democrat-Missouri* [Harrisonville], 30 June 1972 .

"Fourth Death in Harrisonville." *Sedalia Democrat* [Sedalia], 25 Aug. 1972, p. 3.

"Fourth Victim of Wild Shooting Spree Dies."   *Great Bend Tribune* [Great Bend], 25 Apr. 1972, p. 2.

Friends from Harrisonville. "Letter from Hippies to Shelter."May 1972 , Cass County Historical Society, Harrisonville.

"G.M. Allen to Vacate Seat in 122nd District." *The Star Herald*   [Belton, Missouri], 1986.

Gough, Ron. Personal interview with the author. 21 Sept. 2022.

Hackett, Kathryn, Personal Interview with Author. 12 June 2022.

Hamilton, Sergeant G. A. *Missouri State Highway Patrol.*   Harrisonville: Harrisonville Police Dept, 12 April 1972

Hardy, Darlene. "Don Marler." E-mail to the author, 21 Jan. 2023.

"Harrisonville hopes to settle differences." *The Iola Register* [Iola], 29 Apr. 1972, p. 4.

"Harrisonville Hunts for Reason In Terror Spree That Killed 3." *The Springfield Leader and Press* [Springfield], 1972, p. 6.

"Harrisonville Man Innocent." *The Kansas City Times* [Kansas City], 2 June 1972.

Harrisonville Vigilance Committee.   "Letter to Harrisonville Authorities and Merchants." 20   June 1972, Harrisonville Police File, Harrisonville.

Hoke, James. Personal emails with the author. 3 Feb. 2023.

Hood, Richard. "Harrisonville Anxiously Trying to Move Ahead." *Columbia Missourian* [Columbia, Missouri], 8 Aug. 1972.

"Hope to Ease Tensions in Edgy Town." *The Cass County Democrat-Missourian* [Harrisonville], 28 Mar. 1972.

Hutson, Jack. Personal interview with the author. 14 Apr. 2022.

"James Harris Obituary." *Tribute Archive.com*, www.tributearchive.com/obituaries/12327984/Jimmy-Harris. Accessed 17 Sept. 2022.

Jones, Harry, Jr. "Portrait of a Murderer." *The Kansas City Star*   [Kansas City], 26 Apr. 1972.

Jones, Harry, Jr. "Vigilantes Ride Harrisonville Square." *The Kansas City Star* [Kansas City], 25 June 1972, pp. 1+.

Kagarice, Steve. Personal interview with the author. 19 November 2022.

Law Enforcement Assistance Council, compiler. *Harrisonville: A Community in Crisis*. Law Enforcement Assistance Council, Aug. 1972.

"Law Enforcement Ordinances Passed." *The Cass County Democrat-Missourian* [Harrisonville], 21 Mar. 1972.

Leach, John. "Whose Fault?" The Cass County Democrat-Missourian [Harrisonville, Missouri], 12 May 1972. Pg 7A

Leach, Tricia. Personal Text Messages with the author. 10 Feb 2023

Maloney, Janice. Personal Interview with the author. 12 June 2022.

Marler-Hardy, Darlene. Personal emails with the author. 24 Feb. 2023.

Minich, Dennis. "Witnesses recall murders." *The Tribune:South Cass; Bates County*, 21 Apr. 2022.

"New City Ordinance Clarified for Reader." *Wildcat News* [Harrison ville], 12 May 1972.

Nichols, Mike. "A Decade After Shootings On Square, Harrisonville is a Different Place." *The Cass County Democrat-Missourian* [Harris onville], 16 Apr. 1982.

"Not a tranquil time." *The Tribune: South Cass; Bates County*, 21 Apr. 2022.

Orlet, Chris. "charlie simpson's apocalypse: A forgotten masterpiece of new journalism." *Thesmartset.com*, 23 June 2017, 1973whsreun ion.blogspot.com/. Accessed 15 Dec. 2022.

The Pittsburgh Press [Pittsburgh]. 2 Jan. 1974.

"Public Services Are Honored At Wednesday Night Meeting." *Cass County Democrat-Missourian* [Harrisonville], 12 May 1972.

Plotz, David. "Joe Eszterhas How did a B-movie screenwriter become an A-list celebrity?" *Slate.com*, Slate Group, 15 Mar. 1998, www.s late.com/articles/news_and_politics/assessment/1998/03/joe_eszter has.html. Accessed 15 Dec. 2022.

"Police Memorial Fund Totals Over $7,500." *The Cass County Demo crat-Missourian* [Harrisonville], 28 July 1972, pp. 1-2.

"Proposed City Ordinance Causes Local Controversies." *The Wildcat News* [Harrisonville], 7 Apr. 1972.

Raine, Tim. Personal interview with the author. 15 September 2022.

Rorabaugh, W. J. "Hippies Won the Culture War." *History News Net work*, Columbian College of Arts and Sciences, 27 Sept. 2015, hist orynewsnetwork.org/article/160407. Accessed 17 June 2022.

Rousseau, Letha. Personal interview with the author. 9 Nov. 2022.

Simpson-Inman, Rita. Personal interview with the author. 6 Nov. 2022

Smith, Sharon. Personal interview with the author. 30 Oct. 2022.

Street, Janice. Personal interview with the author. 3 May. 2022.

Tammeus, William.   "Black Day in Harrisonville as 3 Dead Laid to Rest." *The Kansas City Star*   [Kansas City], 25 Apr. 1972.

"Terror in a Small Town."   *The San Francisco Chronicle*   [San Fran cisco], 24 Apr. 1972.

"Timothy Leary." *Wikipedia*, WikiMedia Foundation, en.wikipedia.or g/wiki/TimothyLeary. Accessed 7 June 2022.

"Two-Day Clean-Up Project is Held By Youths, Adults." *The Cass County Democrat-Missourian* [Harrisonville], 4 Aug. 1972, p. 1.

Van Meter, Vicki. "Change of park's name heals family: Orville Allen's name added." *The Cass County Democrat-Missourian* [Harrisonville], 1983.

Wardall, G.H., and Ted G. Snyder. "Letters to the Editor." *The Belton Star-Herald* [Belton], 22 June 1972.

"We Want to be Right." *The Cass County Democrat-Missourian* [Harrisonville], 11 Aug. 1972, pp. 4B-4C.

Wilson, Eva. "A 'black day' in Harrisonville." *The Kansas State Collegian* [Manhattan], 16 Apr. 1982.

Wirt, Chris. Personal emails with author. 8 Feb. 2023

Wirt, Dan. Personal interview with author. 10 Jan. 2023.

White, Ray and Connie. Personal interview with the author. 22 Dec. 2022.

Wilks, Ed. "Death and Counter-Culture Come to a Small Town." *St. Louis Post Dispatch* [St. Louis], 7 May 1972, pp. 1+.

"Youth Kills Two Policemen, Takes Own Life." *The Indianapolis Star* [Indianapolis], 24 Apr. 1972, p.43.

Index

About the Author

Jonathan Jones was born and raised in Harrisonville, Missouri. He graduated from Missouri State University with a BS in Business Education and later earned an MBA in International Business from Park University. Jones spent ten years as a teacher and coach in Missouri Schools before moving into the business world where he has spent the next 20+ years working as a business solutions specialist for IAT Insurance Group. Jones is a lifelong history buff and spends much of his spare time researching history, both in his local area as well as traveling to visit historic sites around the world. Jones and his wife of 33 years, Jill, have three grown children, Zac, Lexi, and Nikai and currently live in Olathe, Kansas. More information about Jones' work can be found by visiting www.JonathanJonesAuthor.com .